STRENGTH IN ADVERSITY

The Resourcefulness of American Families in Need

FAMILY SERVICE AMERICA'S 1997 NATIONAL SURVEY OF FAMILIES IN NEED

Funded by Metropolitan Life Foundation

Thomas E. Lengyel, M.S.W., Ph.D.
Christopher Thompson, Ph.D.
Pamela J. Nies!

Family Service America, Inc.
Milwaukee, Wisconsin

ACKNOWLEDGMENTS

Thanks to Metropolitan Life Foundation for supporting this project and the three state focus reports published separately as part of this national research initiative. Metropolitan Life Foundation's commitment to helping families help themselves, as well as its support of Family Service America, was pivotal in the completion of this project.

Also pivotal were the 89 Family Service America member agencies and their staffs who assisted in the field testing, development, and data collection associated with this research. The completion of this report would have been impossible without their dedication and effort. (A full listing of participants can be found in Appendix V.)

Thanks also to Peter Goldberg, FSA president and CEO; Shirley Stewart, president and CEO of Bethany for Children and Families (Moline, Illinois); and Reed Henderson, president and CEO of Family and Children's Service (Richmond, Virginia), for their inspiration and direction behind this project.

Finally, thanks to Ralph Burant and Rebecca Kaegi of Families International's publications division for the editing, design, and production support in the creation of this final report.

ISBN 0-87304-310-3

Copyright 1997 Family Service America, Inc.
Published by Families International, Inc.
11700 West Lake Park Drive
Milwaukee, WI 53224

⬤42   Printed in the United States

STRENGTH IN ADVERSITY
The Resourcefulness of American Families in Need

TABLE OF CONTENTS

The need for periodic assessments of family status
Background and history of the National Survey
Brief summary of methodology
Innovative features of the 1997 survey

Age, gender, ethnicity
Family structure
Economic status

Breakdown by social and economic categories
Comparison with 1990 data

Relationship to consumer characteristics
Relationship to consumer problems
Appropriateness, degree of fit, and specificity of
service response

Importance of public resources to recipients
and nonrecipients
Characteristics of public assistance recipients
vs. nonrecipients
Problems and services for recipients vs. nonrecipients
Policy implications

LIST OF TABLES AND FIGURES

LIST OF TABLES

LIST OF FIGURES

1. EXECUTIVE SUMMARY

■ The 1997 survey reached 10,000 individuals and families who had contact with family service agencies in 26 states and the District of Columbia

■ Family service agencies have shifted toward serving a marginalized population of consumers

■ Most people seeking professional help report problems in their *social relations*, but a rapidly growing group have problems providing for their *basic needs*

■ Services have not kept pace with changes in the problems people report, resulting in a general mismatch between service delivery and community needs

■ Patterns of resource use contradict the conventional wisdom that marginalized individuals and families are isolated from social resources

■ People use a healthy mix of friends, neighbors, and kin, as well as professional support, to cope with life

■ Consumer reliance on agency and institutional resources appears to influence their valuation of the helpfulness of friends, neighbors, and kin

■ Individuals who experience greater stress, including women and welfare recipients, appear to make greater use of their social resources

■ Underutilized assets represent enormous potential for family service agencies to assess and broker on the basis of strengths rather than deficits

Family Service America's 1997 National Survey replicated studies conducted at 10-year intervals since 1970, but enhanced the methodology to include assessment of family strengths and appraisal of the accuracy of social workers' knowledge about the consumers who seek their professional services. Its purpose was to document changes that have affected the American family since 1990 and to provide a national baseline against which local conditions and future surveys could be com-

2. Introduction

Organizations whose purpose is the betterment of families and the communities in which they live are effective to the degree that their strategies and plans are founded on accurate knowledge of the conditions of life of those families and communities. This constraint motivates the periodic reassessment of the quality of life of the American family, in broad scope. Family Service America (FSA) has conducted national surveys of the American family at 10-year intervals since 1970, the most recent of which was completed in 1990. The results were published as *American Families in Trouble* (Haas & Wahl, 1991).

Since the publication of that report, anecdotal observations from social service professionals across the country suggest that the problems experienced by the consumers they served were growing more numerous, more extensive, and more severe. On this basis, with support from the Metropolitan Life Foundation, FSA resolved to implement a new national survey before the end of the decade. The present survey was designed to serve four basic purposes:

- Document changes that have affected the family since 1990
- Establish a national and state baseline of consumer profiles for comparison with future surveys
- Provide the national and state norms against which current local community and agency profiles can be viewed
- Encourage agencies and their staffs to assess their consumers and develop programming on the basis of strengths rather than deficits

To implement these goals, FSA conducted a cross-sectional study of consumers served by its member agencies across the United States. These agencies are nonprofit social service and mental health organizations rooted in local communities. A parallel study was coordinated in Canada in collaboration with Family Service Canada. The design called for administering the survey to all consumers who received face-to-face professional services of any kind from the staff members of participating agencies during the seven-day period April 7–13. To preserve comparability with the 1990 survey data, the 1997 instrument included the 1990 instrument almost verbatim, modified only by minor updates in the inventory of problems and services. This part of the instrument (Part I) was completed by the direct service provider at the time of contact with the consumer. (A detailed description of the methodology is offered in Appendix 1 and the full instrument appears in Appendix 2.)

The present survey was designed to encourage social service agencies and their staffs to assess their consumers and develop programming on the basis of strengths instead of weaknesses or deficits.

The 1997 survey also embodied major innovations. In particular, the survey included a new means of assessing the strengths of consumers, known as the Assets Inventory. This instrument was developed specifically to capture the variety of resources used by consumers in going about their daily lives and to allow consumers to characterize resources they had used in terms of degree of helpfulness. It was a self-administered instrument, completed by the consumer (Part II-B). Furthermore, in order to assess the accuracy of the knowledge base of social service and mental health professionals about the consumers they serve, the survey design required service providers independently to complete an Assets Inventory on the consumer being surveyed, based on their prior knowledge or assessment (Part II-A). The three parts of a single instrument all bore the same unique identifying number to facilitate matching survey parts that inadvertently became disarticulated. Unique, sequential numbering of instruments facilitated tracking of surveys and program- or site-level analysis within agencies.

In 1990, 16,446 individuals and families were surveyed at 85 agencies in 31states, the District of Columbia, and British Columbia. The more complex 1997 survey reached 9,938 individuals and families at 89 agencies spread across 26 states and the District of Columbia. The Canadian version of the 1997 survey reached 1,450 individuals at 26 agencies in 9 provinces. The Canadian data are analyzed separately. A joint comparative report is planned. The geographic breakdown of completed surveys appears as Appendix 3.

3. Characteristics of Consumers Surveyed

The 1997 National Survey asked for consumer information on a variety of individual and family characteristics: age, gender, ethnicity, marital status, education, employment status, occupation, place of residence, and family income as well as age, gender, and relationship of others making up the consumer's household.

3.1 Geographic distribution of completed survey instruments

Summary findings

■ 9,938 completed survey instruments were received from 89 agencies in 26 states and the District of Columbia, representing all regions of the country.

■ Responses were weighted to the northeast with just three of these states contributing one-third of the total.

■ The population served by FSA agencies is more urban than the general population of the United States.

Detailed findings

In the 1997 survey, 9,938 completed forms were returned from 89 FSA member agencies in 26 states and the District of Columbia, across all four regions of the country.[1] The Northeast and the South contributed more than one-third of the total each, whereas the Midwest yielded only 17% and the West less than 6% of cases (see Figure 1).

---

1. The four U.S. Bureau of the Census regions are: Northeast (ME, NH, NY, PA, VT, MA, RI, CT, and NJ), Midwest (ND, MN, SD, NE, KS, IA, MO, WI, IL, MI, IN, and OH), South (DE, MD, DC, VA, WV, KY, NC, TN, AR, OK, TX, LA, MS, AL, SC, GA, and FL), and West (AK, WA, OR, CA, ID, NV, MT, WY, UT, CO, AZ, NM, and HI).

Geographic Distribution of Respondents
By Distribution of U.S. Population

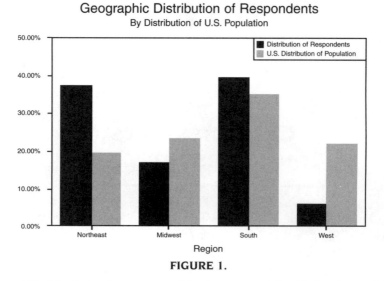

FIGURE 1.

The Northeast is represented in the survey at double its share of the national population, whereas the West is underrepresented. The most surveys from a single state was 1,375 (13.8% of the total) from New Jersey. The second most prominent state was Connecticut, with 1,288 surveys (13%). Pennsylvania was the only other state contributing more than 10% of the total. These three states are also the only states that returned more than 1,000 completed forms each; together they account for slightly more than one third of the survey total (3,671 forms, or 36.9%). More than 100 completed forms were returned by each of 19 states and the District of Columbia. The fewest number of forms from a single state was 3, from Kansas.

Respondents were asked about their place of residence (i.e., city, suburb, rural town, or rural farm). The majority of consumers (58%) are city dwellers; only 13.4% live in rural areas. Almost one-third (28.6%) live in a suburban area. Compared with the U.S. population as a whole, a greater share of the surveyed group lives in urban areas (86.6% compared with 75.2%), whereas a smaller share lives in rural areas (13.4% compared to 24.8% nationally).

3.2 CONSUMER AGE AND GENDER

Summary findings

■ The consumer group, on average, is younger than the U.S. population, with a smaller share of seniors.

■ Female consumers outnumber males about 2 to 1 overall: females are more likely to be clustered in the young-adult and senior age groups, whereas males are more likely to be grouped in the older-adult and child-age groups.

Detailed findings

The average age of consumers served by FSA agencies in this survey is 32.9 years, with a greater share of younger people than in the population as a whole: 60.2% of those surveyed are younger than 35 years compared with 51.2% across the United States.[2] Surveyed seniors represent only half their proportion in the U.S. population: 6.4% of the surveyed group are 65 years or older compared with 12.7% of the general population. Males in the group have a younger average age (29.9 years) than the U.S. average for males, whereas females have a higher average age (34.2 years) than the U.S. average for females, at 28.3%. Females outnumber males in the surveyed group, as they do in the population as a whole, but the share of females in the surveyed group (65.2%) is much higher than in the general population (51.2%). The largest grouping of male consumers (28.3%) is in the older-adult range (35–49 years), whereas the largest group of females (33.1%) is in the younger-adult age range (20–34 years). Males are more clustered than females in the child and adolescent age groups: 36.8% of male consumers are younger than 20 years compared with 24.7% of females. Females are more prominent in the senior (older than 65 years) group, which accounts for 7.3% of all female consumers, compared with only 3.8% of all male consumers. Generally speaking, women are overrepresented in the older age ranges at the FSA agencies participating in the 1997 survey. Males are overrepresented in the youngest age classes (younger than 20 years). (See Figure 2).

3.3 MARITAL STATUS

Summary findings

■ Slightly more than half of all respondents are single, and one in four is married.

■ These consumers are much more likely to be single or divorced and much less likely to be married than the U.S. population as a whole.

---

2. For purposes of comparison with U.S. census data, age categories have been recoded in the following discussion. Comparisons with 1990 survey data employ the original age categories.

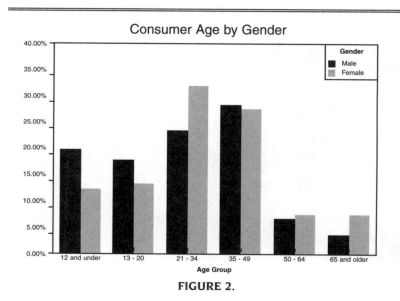

Consumer Age by Gender

Gender
■ Male
■ Female

Age Group

FIGURE 2.

Detailed findings

Service providers recorded the consumer's marital status, and the answers were classified as single, married, separated/divorced, widowed, living together unmarried, or other. Slightly more than half of all adult clients (51.1%) are described as single. The next most frequent status is married (26.1%), followed by 17.4% separated/divorced; only 5.1% are widowed.

Comparison with the frequency of different marital statuses in the adult U.S. population as a whole cannot be precise, because the *Annual Abstract of Statistics* groups people differently. Not withstanding these complexities, one can say that consumers at FSA agencies are almost twice as likely to be either single or a member of an unmarried couple (51.4% of consumers) compared with the U.S. population as a whole. Further, the consumer group is almost twice as likely as the general population to be separated/divorced (17.4% here compared with 9.2% nationally). In sum, those served by participating FSA agencies are much less likely to be married than Americans in general (26.1% compared with 60.9% nationally).

3.4 FAMILY SIZE AND STRUCTURE
Summary findings

■ The average family size is 2.37 people per case, but almost half the cases had only one individual.

■ A large number of family types could be distinguished, with single adults and couples each accounting for one-quarter of cases.

■ Traditional nuclear families with two parents and children account for only 1 in 10 cases.

■ Females greatly outnumber males in the single-parent and widowed categories.

Detailed findings

The FSA survey instrument asked service providers to enter information on other members of the consumer's household. This information included relationship to the consumer, age, and gender for all household members, up to a total of 10 members. This information can be sorted to give the simple distribution of family size[3] and types among the surveyed consumers and can also be used later to assess differences in age and income between different family types (see Table 1).

In terms of family size, the mean number of individuals across all cases with information is 2.37 people, and the median family size is 2.0, which is slightly smaller than in 1990. This signals an increase in the

TABLE 1.

Distribution of Family Structures			
Family Structure	**Percent (n)**	**Family Structure**	**Percent (n)**
Single Nonwidowed:	28.7% (2397)	Couple With Parent:	0.5% (48)
Males	8.9% (747)	No Children	0.2% (19)
Females	15.7% (1311)	And Children	0.3% (29)
Gender Unknown	4.1% (339)	Single With Parent:	6.6% (552)
Single Parents:	13.5% (1131)	No Children	5.7% (473)
Males	1.1% (96)	And Children	0.9% (79)
Females	10.6% (885)	Sibling - No Partner:	12.1% (1007)
Gender Unknown	1.8% (150)	No Children	11.2% (938)
Married Couples:	26.2% (2180)	With Children	0.8% (69)
Without Children	6.3% (523)	Widowed:	4.8% (399)
With Children	11.0% (921)	Male	0.6% (49)
Listed Alone	8.8% (736)	Female	3.2% (267)
Unmarried Couples:	0.0% (6)	Gender Unknown	1.0% (83)
Without Children	0.0% (4)	Children Listed Alone	7.6% (632)
With Children	0.0% (2)		

3. The term "family" is used here to denote any case with more than just the individual consumer listed on the same form and is not defined by any actual legal relations between those individuals.

number of single persons served since 1990. In 1997, almost half the returned forms (4,508 cases, or 46%) had the consumer listed as the only member of the household. Only 6% of forms show more than five individuals in the family, and extremely large family groupings (seven or more individuals present on a survey form) account for slightly more than 1% of all cases. For the reasons given below, we believe this overcounts single individual households.

The information on relatives allows 8,352 cases (84% of the total) to be allocated to 1 of 21 different types of family. These fall into one of seven larger groups, according to the major differentiating dimensions of single/couple, children/no children, siblings, and widowed.

Results show that no single type of family is in the majority. The most prevalent major family type is single nonwidowed adults. Singles account for more than a quarter of the cases (28.7%). Within this type, single females (15.7% of all cases) are almost twice as prevalent as single males (8.9%). The next most frequent grouping is couples (both married and unmarried), which accounts for 26.7% of all cases. Less than half (11%) of these couples are married with children, and 6.3% are married without children. Another 8.8% report their status as married but are listed alone on the form. The traditional nuclear family unit, married with child(ren), accounts for only about 1 in 10 cases (11%). Single parents account for 13.5% of those surveyed and this group is made up of far more single female parents (10.6% of respondents) than single male parents (1.1% of respondents). Females are also more prevalent in the widowed group, in which they account for 3.2% within the 4.8% widowed subtotal.

3.5 CONSUMER ETHNICITY

Summary findings

■ Two-thirds of consumers are white and one-third are minorities.

■ African Americans account for one in five cases, which is double their representation in the population as a whole and almost double their share in 1990.

Detailed findings

Consumer ethnicity was classified into one of six categories in 1997 (White, Hispanic, African American, Asian, Native American, and other). Approximately two-thirds (67%) of the survey respondents are White and one-third are minorities, compared with three-quarters White (75.3%) and one-quarter minorities in the U.S. population as a whole. The largest minority group in the survey is African American, which accounts for 22.5% of all cases. This is almost double the African American representation in the U.S. population as a whole. Asians, Hispanics, and Native Americans each are less represented among respondents than in the U.S. population. The population served by participating FSA agencies therefore includes considerably more minorities than the U.S. population as a whole, primarily because these agencies are serving a much higher proportion of African Americans.

Since 1990, the population served by FSA agencies appears to have become increasingly impoverished.

Compared with the 1990 survey group, African Americans have almost doubled their share as consumers, rising from 12.3% of all cases to 22.5%, while Whites have declined from 79.6% of all cases to 67%. Hispanics increased their share slightly, from 4.6% to 6.6%, and the Asian share decreased, from 3.4% to .6% of cases.

3.6 CONSUMER EDUCATION

Summary findings

- One in six consumers lacks a high school diploma or GED.
- 55.1% have achieved a high school diploma or GED.
- Slightly more than one-third of consumers has more than a high school education.
- One in six FSA consumers has a college degree.

Detailed findings

Service providers gave information about the educational level of the people they served, writing in the consumer's educational attainment. Slightly more than one in six (17.8%) had not gained a high school diploma or GED. About the same proportion (17.5%) had a college degree. In between are 19.6% with some college or with technical school education or certification. If we define "education that can get a basic job" as having at least a high school degree or GED, then a large majority of consumers (82.2%) has it. On the other hand, if we define "education that gets a job" as any level completed beyond high school, then only slightly more than one-third of the surveyed group has it.

3.7 CONSUMER EMPLOYMENT STATUS

Summary findings

■ Less than half of consumers served by FSA agencies has full-time employment.

■ Males are more likely to be employed full time and females are more likely to be employed part time.

■ Females are more likely to be unemployed than males.

Detailed findings

The survey instrument asked the service provider to characterize the consumer's employment status. Only a minority of consumers (42.2%) has full-time employment, although full-time employment is higher for males (48.3%) than it is for females (39.8%). Conversely, females are more likely to have part-time employment (7.9%) than males (4.7%) and are more likely to be unemployed (31.0%) than are males (19.5%). Slightly more than half of males (53%) and less than half of females (47.7%) have either part-time or full-time employment (see Figure 3).

Being employed (both full time or part time) and being unemployed (i.e., in the work force) account for 75.9% of cases. Of the balance, 14.4% are students. Males are almost twice as likely (20.3% of

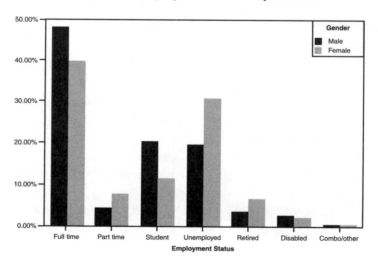

Consumer Employment Status by Gender

FIGURE 3.

20

all male cases) to be students as females (11.6% of ‹
The retired group accounts for 6.4% of all cases and
be females than males (6.7% of all females compared
males). Disabled consumers account for 2.6% of all

3.8 CONSUMER INCOME

Summary findings

■ Median income for households surveyed is $14,800, which is less
than half the national median income.

■ The share of cases in the lowest income category has more than
doubled since 1990.

■ Couples have the highest average income, and single parents and
widoweds have the lowest.

Detailed findings

The average family income for all cases that have this information
is $20,997 a year, and the median is $14,800. (The median is more rep-
resentative of all cases; the difference indicates the mean has been
skewed upwards by the presence of a few high-income cases). This
median figure is less than half (45.9%) the dollar value of the most
recently available median income figure for all households in the United States ($32,264 in 1994). This demonstrates that consumers served

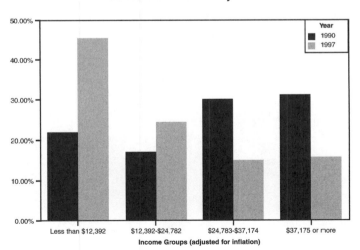

Consumer Income by Year

FIGURE 4.

rticipating FSA agencies are much poorer, on average, than the pulation of the country as a whole.

When cases are grouped according to the same income categories used in the 1990 survey (adjusted for inflation), almost half are in the lowest category of less than $12,392 per year. This category has seen the largest growth relative to the others between the times of the two surveys. In 1990, only 22% of cases in the survey were in the lowest income category, compared with 45.2% in 1997. The next lowest category has also grown, from 17.0% to 24.4% of cases, while the share of cases in the two upper categories (more than $24,783 a year in 1997) has declined by half—from 61% of all cases in 1990 to 30.5% in 1997. In other words, since 1990, the population served by FSA agencies appears to have become increasingly impoverished (see Figure 4).

Family income also varies by family type. Cases in the "couples" (married and unmarried) family type have an average income equal to 156% of the surveyed group as a whole. Single parents, on average, have an average income that is much lower than that for all cases (at 66.3% of the average) and lower than that for singles without children (at 72.1% of the average). Cases in the widowed group have the lowest average income of any family group (43.2% of the average for all cases), and widowed females within this group have the lowest average income (40.3% of the average for all cases).

4. Consumer
Needs and Problems

- Parenting and child-rearing issues led the field of presenting problems.
- A broad group of social-relational issues dominated other functional areas.

Comparing 1990 results with those of 1997 in terms of *changes* in problems:

- The proportion of people seeking help for marital issues continued its pattern of decline since 1970.
- 1997 results demonstrate a dramatic shift in consumer problems toward a focus on basic needs.
- Street-level problems (abuse and violence, criminal and delinquent behavior) increase substantially.
- Protective service issues grow significantly.
- Relationships with children are of increasing concern.

4.1 The menu of problems

The 1990 survey offered 38 choices for identifying the "presenting problems" of the consumers who were seeking help. These were itemized under four headings on the survey instrument:

- Family relationships
- Personality adjustment
- Other problems
- Need for physical care or protective service

The service professional who completed this section of the survey was asked to check all problems reported and to indicate which of these was the most important. An individual consumer could be characterized as having more than one presenting problem. Three lines were provided to write in "other" problems not captured in the survey menu. As a result of field testing in February and March of 1997, the problem categories Domestic Violence and Neglect were added to the problem menu for the 1997 survey.

The set of problems that brought people into family service agencies in 1997 is dominated by parent–child relationships (under the Family Relationships heading). More than a third (35.1%) of consumers reported this relationship as one of the presenting problems for which they were seeking services. Of all choices, it was also the category most commonly cited as "most important" (3.2% of survey answers). Supporting these concerns, parenting/child-rearing problems were cited (under the heading Other Problems) as a problem in more than one-quarter (27.4%) of responses. The frequency of this latter category matches very closely the survey results from 1970 and 1990, so there was essentially no change in the standing of the parenting/child-rearing issue as a portion of the total problem set.

The 1997 survey offers other strong evidence that relationships with children generally were the central issue in the lives of these families. Two problem areas in which children are key players—school-related problems (17.5%) and single-parenting problems (16.4%)—were near the top of the list.

4.2 PROBLEM GROUPS

We reconfigured all of the presenting problems into four broad types (see Table 2). Parent–child relationships are part of a complex set of issues that can be considered *social-relational*. This group also includes the following:

- Abuse/violence
- Single parenting
- Divorce
- Work-related problems
- Teen parenting
- Stepparenting

- Problems in social contacts
- Domestic violence
- Criminal or delinquent behaviors
- Neglect
- Unwed parenting

This set of issues clearly dominated the menu of problems. More than three of five consumers (61.4%) sought service for a problem within this functional area.[4]

---

4. Because consumers could report more than one problem—and many of them did so—the percentages for the various problems shown in Table 2, as well as for the four functional problem groups, add up to more than 100%.

TABLE 2.

"OTHER PROBLEM" GROUPINGS IN THE NATIONAL SURVEY
Ranked by Frequency Within Groups

Social/relational (61.4%)	Basic Needs (35.8%)	Mental Health (27.9%)	Other/situational (38.2%)
Parenting/child rearing (27.4%)	Inadequate income for basic needs (15.9%)	Mental illness (12.8%)	School-related problems (17.5%)
Abuse/violence (18.6%)	Physical health problems (13.8%)	Alcoholism (11.5%)	Money management (14.2%)
Problems in social contacts (17.4%)	Housing problems (12.5%)	Drug abuse (9.8%)	Legal problems (10.2%)
Single parenting (16.4%)	Unemployment (11.3%)	Mental retardation/ developmental disability (2.7%)	Problems with leisure time (8.7%)
Domestic violence (12.3 %)	Home management (7.7%)		
Divorce (10.6%)	Handicapped (3.5%)		
Criminal or delinquent behaviors (8.2%)			
Work-related problems (7.6%)			
Neglect (5.4%)			
Teen parenting (4.2%)			
Unwed parenting (3.6%)			
Stepparenting (3.5%)			

Problems related to *basic needs* were strongly represented for the first time in the 1997 survey. This set included the following:

- Inadequate income for basic needs
- Physical health problems
- Housing problems
- Unemployment
- Management of home

Issues such as housing, employment, and inadequate income played a relatively small role in the lives of consumers using FSA agencies in 1990. In 1990, for example, 8.5% of consumers reported

25

housing as an issue. By 1997 this group had grown by nearly 50%, with 12.5% needing help with housing. The importance of inadequate income as a problem increased from 13.3% to 15.9% in the same period, despite the fact that the national employment picture improved. Between April 1990 and April 1997, national unemployment dropped from 5.4% to 4.9%. Overall, in 1997, approximately three of eight consumers (35.8%) were seeking help from these agencies for basic needs. Some of these individuals and families also sought help for problems in the other functional areas. These figures suggest that by 1997 FSA agencies had begun to recruit a more marginalized group of consumers, who were left behind by the national economic recovery.

By 1997, FSA *agencies had begun recruiting a more marginalized group of consumers who were left behind by the national economic recovery.*

Mental health was another major functional area well represented in the 1997 responses. Of those surveyed, 27.9% reported a problem in this area. This group included mental illness (mentioned as a problem in 12.8% of contacts), alcoholism (11.5%), drug abuse (9.8%), and mental retardation (2.7%).

The last functional area might be termed *situational/other*, in which 38.2% of respondents were seeking help for one of the following issues: school-related problems (17.5%), money management (14.2%), legal problems (10.2%), or problems with leisure time (8.7%). The high frequency of school-related problems in the database is almost certainly the result of including participants in the Families and Schools Together (FAST) programs in the survey population. Family Service America has been actively promoting FAST as a model early-intervention program for at-risk children in grades K through 6 during the past four years. The program has taken root at more than 300 sites across the country, many of which were represented in the survey.

4.3 CHANGES IN CONSUMER PROBLEMS SINCE 1990

A primary purpose in replicating the 1990 survey instrument was to facilitate comparisons with the data it provided. The following comparisons emerged readily from the 1990 and 1997 databases (see Table 3, pages 27 and 28).

In 1997, approximately one in five people (20.6%) who were served at these agencies was concerned with marital issues. This repre-

TABLE 3.

CHANGES IN THE FREQUENCY OF REPORTED PROBLEMS
1990 TO 1997

PROBLEMS *INCREASING*	1990 FREQUENCY	1997 FREQUENCY	NET CHANGE
Abuse/violence & domestic violence	22.1 %	30.9 %	8.8 %
Need for physical care/protective service-child & neglect	4.6 %	12.7 %	8.1 %
Family relationships: other	8.8 %	16.5 %	7.7 %
Other problem - 1 (write-in)	12.9 %	20.1 %	7.2 %
Housing	8.5 %	12.5 %	4.0 %
Single parenting	12.6 %	16.4 %	3.8 %
Family relationships: parent-child	32.1 %	35.1 %	3.0 %
Inadequate income for basic needs	13.3 %	15.9 %	2.6 %
School related	15.6 %	17.5 %	1.9 %
Criminal or delinquent behaviors	6.3 %	8.2 %	1.9 %
Mental illness	11.1 %	12.8 %	1.7 %
Need for physical care/protective service-youth	2.3 %	3.9 %	1.6 %
Legal problems	8.9 %	10.2 %	1.3 %
Teen parenting	2.9 %	4.2 %	1.3 %
Unwed parenting	2.4 %	3.6 %	1.2 %
Mental retardation	2.0 %	2.7 %	0.7 %
Unemployment	10.9 %	11.3 %	0.4 %
Personality adjustment-youth	10.7 %	10.9 %	0.2 %
Need for physical care/protective service-adult	1.7 %	1.9 %	0.2 %
Parenting/child rearing	27.3 %	27.4 %	0.1 %

sents a further decline from the level documented in 1990 (25%), and a dramatic decline since the first national survey in 1970, when about 48% of individuals sought help for marital issues. This change is consistent with the changing characteristics of the customer base. In 1990, approximately three of eight (36.6%) consumers were married, whereas by 1997 only two of eight (26.1%) were married.

What might be termed "street level" problems increased significantly among consumers served by FSA agencies over 1990 levels.

What might be termed "street level" problems increased significantly among consumers served by FSA agencies in 1997 compared

PROBLEMS *UNCHANGED*	1990 FREQUENCY	1997 FREQUENCY	NET CHANGE
Drug abuse	9.8 %	9.8 %	0 %
Problems with leisure time	8.7 %	8.7 %	0 %
PROBLEMS *DECREASING*	**1990 FREQUENCY**	**1997 FREQUENCY**	**NET CHANGE**
Handicapped	3.6 %	3.5 %	- 0.1 %
Problems in social contacts	17.8 %	17.4 %	- 0.4 %
Personality adjustment-child	10.5 %	10.1 %	-0.4 %
Stepparenting	4.3 %	3.5 %	- 0.8 %
Other-3 (write-in) [various]	1.5 %	0.7 %	- 0.8 %
Personality adjustment-aged	3.2 %	2.0 %	- 1.2 %
Management of money	15.5 %	14.2 %	- 1.3 %
Other-2 (write-in) [various]	4.7 %	3.2 %	- 1.5 %
Need for physical care/protective services-aged	3.9 %	2.3 %	- 1.6 %
Divorce	14.1 %	10.6 %	- 3.5 %
Physical health problems	17.7 %	13.8 %	- 3.9 %
Management of home	12.0 %	7.7 %	- 4.3 %
Family relationships-marital	25.6 %	20.6 %	- 5.0 %
Work-related problems	13.3 %	7.6 %	- 5.7 %
Alcoholism	18.7 %	11.5 %	- 7.2 %
Personality adjustment-adult	35.0 %	16.9 %	- 18.1 %

with 1990. Abuse/violence, domestic violence, criminal and delinquent behaviors, and legal problems increased as a group by 12% relative to 1990. If one includes the problems associated with single, teen, and unwed parenting, the increase is 18.3% relative to 1990. The contrast with the more traditional array of problems served by FSA agencies in prior years will become clearer in the following discussion of problem areas that have subsided.

Consistent with the growth of street issues, protective service problems became more prominent. The need for physical or protective services for children, youth, and adults (but not the aged) grew by nearly 10% during the past seven years. A comparable increase was manifest in the basic needs area, wherein housing, inadequate income, and unemployment were more commonly reported in 1997 (greater by 7%) than in 1990.

Finally, problems in relationships with children also showed a noticeable increase in this seven-year span. A group that includes family relationships—parent–child, personality adjustment-youth, and parenting/child rearing—evinces a 3.3% rise. This understates the augmented importance of this functional area, in that many issues with children are folded into the areas with large increases (e.g., single parenting).

In contrast, many traditional concerns addressed by counseling agencies declined substantially in the period between the two surveys. Problems of personality adjustment for children, the aged, and adults, declined by a fifth (19.7%). Individuals and families seeking help with divorce or marital problems dropped by 8.5%. And problems of the aged—personality adjustment, need for protective services, physical health problems, and management of home—declined by 11%. In general, a decline in issues predominantly experienced by the middle class is documented in the 1997 survey.

5. SERVICES
OFFERED TO CONSUMERS

5.1 THE SERVICE MENU

The 1997 National Survey of the American Family asked providers to check any of 34 possible service lines that they had recommended for consumers. (For the full list of options, see the survey instrument in Appendix 2). Analysis of these responses pursued two paths:

■ The current frequency of individual services and common patterns of provision, along with any changes in these areas since the last survey in 1990

■ The link between these services and the kinds of problems consumers are presenting

The relationship to problems can be made on an individual service-line basis as well as by sorting problems into the major functional groups described above: relational, basic needs, mental health, and situational/other. The second strategy allows us to see what kinds of services have been offered to consumers whose reported problems fall into only one functional group.

5.2 THE FREQUENCY OF DIFFERENT KINDS OF SERVICES

Summary findings

■ Counseling is offered to two-thirds of all cases.

■ Counseling has declined in frequency since 1990, when 72.4% of consumers received it.

■ Only two other services—psychiatric clinic and support group—are given to more than 10% of consumers. Their frequency is still much lower than that of counseling.

Detailed findings

The most frequent service offered by providers to consumers is *counseling*, which is the service plan for 66% of all cases. The second most commonly provided service, *psychiatric or mental health clinic*, is offered to only 14.5% of consumers. *Support group* is the third most frequent service (13.4%). It is the only other service of the 34 that is offered to more than 10% of the consumers. Fully 20 out of the 34 service possibilities are being offered to fewer than 3% of the total consumers. The overall pattern, therefore, is one of service provision being concentrated in the counseling area, and a wide but very thin dispersal of consumers across all the other service possibilities.

Diversification in service delivery appears to lag behind the significant diversification in the characteristics of consumers and their issues.

When this 1997 pattern is compared to the 1990 pattern of services (see Table 4), counseling and psychiatric/mental health clinic are still the top two services by frequency, although the share of total cases receiving counseling is lower by 6.4% in 1997. In both years, only three services are given to more than 10% of clients. Considering those services given to more than 5% of the consumers (a group of 10 services in 1990 and 12 in 1997), *homemaker services* and *elder care* slipped from the top ten between 1990 and 1997, while *child care, family advocacy*, and *credit counseling* enter the top ten in 1997. Overall, 20 service categories increased in their frequency, and 17 decreased. As a general finding, services in 1997 were less concentrated in the top categories and thus were more evenly distributed among service options. This finding is reflected in the social workers' relatively frequent use of

TABLE 4.

Comparison of Top Five Service Plans Offered in 1990 and 1997

1990		1997	
Service Plan	**Percent (*n*)**	**Service Plan**	**Percent (*n*)**
Counseling	72.4% (11902)	Counseling	66.0% (6560)
Psychiatric/Mental Health	14.5% (2378)	Psychiatric/Mental Health	14.5% (1443)
Substance Abuse	10.1% (1665)	Support Group	13.4% (1327)
Child Abuse	7.9% (1296)	Child Care	8.0% (793)
Homemaker Service	7.7% (1274)	Domestic Violence	7.5% (744)
		Substance Abuse	7.5% (744)

the first "other" category (at 9.4%) to describe service plans not listed on the survey menu of services. Our finding here is consistent with the earlier description of consumer characteristics and problems and testifies to the agencies' attempts to adapt their service delivery to a more diverse clientele with a more diverse problem set. Diversification in service delivery, however, appears to lag behind the significant diversification in the characteristics of consumers and their issues.

5.3 THE LINK BETWEEN SERVICES AND PROBLEMS

Summary findings

■ Counseling is the service most frequently provided, regardless of major substantive problem type.

■ The prominence of counseling is muted in the basic needs and other problem functional groups.

■ The pattern of change in services since 1990 does not parallel the changes in consumers' expressed needs, suggesting that service delivery has been molded by other forces, such as funding mechanisms and changes in clientele.

■ Divergence between growth in need and slower growth in corresponding service presents opportunities for expansion.

Detailed findings

Table 5 shows the frequency of services provided for consumers in each of the four broad classes whose presenting problems fall exclusively into one problem group (e.g., basic needs).[5] Examining the services provided to such groups of consumers affords a perspective on the appropriateness of those services. Several points are worth noting.

First, each problem group, regardless of its core substantive nature—relationships, basic needs, mental health, and other—still shows counseling as the most frequent service.

Second, as with all cases in the survey, the pattern of services for those consumers with relationship problems or mental health problems exclusively shows a similar fall off in frequency of service after the most widely prescribed service (counseling). For example, in the relationship-problems group, 80.9% of cases received counseling, but only 11.8% received the next most common service.

---

5. Frequencies of services provided may add up to more than 100% because an individual consumer may be offered more than one service.

TABLE 5.

Service Plan Responses for Consumers With Problems Exclusively in One Problem Group

Rank	Relationship Group			Basic Needs Group			Mental Health Group			Situational/other Group		
	Service Plan	%	n	Service Plan	%	n	Service Plan	%	n	Service Plan	%	n
1	Counseling	80.9	1,257	Counseling	36.8	158	Counseling	71.6	242	Counseling	44.2	167
2	Domestic violence	11.8	183	Elder care/ supportive services	20.5	88	Mental health clinic	26.0	88	Credit counseling	34.9	132
3	Support group	9.6	149	Homemaker service	17.2	74	Substance-abuse services	19.2	65	Mental health clinic	4.8	18
4	Mental health clinic	7.7	120	Home health service	13.1	56	Support group	16.0	54	Support group	3.2	12
5	Child abuse or neglect	6.1	95	Support group	7.9	34	Day-care service for adults	3.8	13	Family advocacy	2.4	9
6	Child care	5.3	82	Services for persons with HIV	7.7	33	Services for developmentally disabled	3.8	13	Foster placement for children	2.4	9

Third, however, this prominence of counseling and the decline in frequency of other services after it was not anywhere near as pronounced for the other two problem groups. In other words, service response for the basic needs and situational consumer groups is more even handed. For the basic needs group, counseling went to only 36.8% of the consumers, while elder care/supportive services to aging went to 20.5% of cases. Similarly, for the "other" problem group, counseling went to 44.2% but credit counseling still went to 34.9%. This pattern offers clear evidence, if indeed any was needed, that service delivery is not merely categorical, but adapts itself to the characteristics of those served.

The service-delivery system at FSA agencies clearly has the ability to change. Almost all categories of service showed nontrivial levels of change over the time punctuated by the two surveys. The fact that social workers resorted to the "other" category to write in their service plans more than 10% of the time demonstrates that the variety of services currently being offered at these agencies far outstripped the inventory designed in 1990 and before to capture them.

The greatest change was in a new category of service first appearing on the 1997 survey: support groups. They were offered as a service plan in 13.4% of contacts in 1997. In fact, the greatest increases among services appear in those that are delivered in group or congregate formats. In addition to support groups, these include child care (up 4.0%), credit counseling (up 1.1%), and day-care service for adults (up .7%). Conversely, many of the services that have declined in frequency appear to be labor intensive, one-on-one interventions, such as counseling (down 6.4%), elder care (down 3.7%), and child abuse and neglect services (down 2.0%).

The pattern of change in services, moreover, does not parallel the change in consumers' expressed needs. If the optimal service response to a problem is a service that is narrowly targeted or tailored to that problem, rather than a generic response that encompasses several problems, then we would expect clearly paired problems and services to rise and fall more or less in step (regardless of whether they were originally in balance). Ideally, a large increase in the incidence of a reported problem (i.e., in demand for a service) should be matched by a perhaps slightly delayed large increase in the frequency of its matched service response.

The 1990 and 1997 survey data provide a good basis for comparing the magnitude of changes in problems with the magnitude of changes in matched services. Abuse and domestic violence together yielded the largest increase of any problem category listed in the survey, an 8.8% gain in frequency. Essential service responses might include emergency shelter, protective service, and domestic violence services, all listed on the service menu. However, these services together showed a net increase of only .8%.[6] Need for child protective services or neglect services increased by 8.1%, nearly as much as abuse and domestic violence. But the logical categories of service response—foster placement, protective service (of all kinds), and child abuse and neglect services—together *decreased* by 0.1%. Single parenting was another major problem category that saw significant growth (3.8%) during the past seven years. Yet, one of the apparently appropriate responses—family life education—saw a 1.7% *decrease*. Finally, housing problems jumped 4.0%. Service for the homeless and emergency shelter services together increased only 1.0%.

On the flip side of this comparison, we can examine problems that showed significant declines in frequency. Divorce as a presenting problem shrank by 3.5% between 1990 and 1997. Divorce mediation showed less of a decline (0.4%). Physical health problems were reported 3.9% less frequently in 1997. Matching service responses—home health services and managed care programs—declined by a net of 1.6%.[7] Money management problems declined 1.3%, whereas credit counseling as a provided service actually *increased* 1.1%.

The trend toward group-delivered services and away from labor-intensive interventions, coupled with the distinct patterns of change that differentiate presenting problems and service responses, together argue that forces other than the expressed needs of consumers are driving changes in service mix and service method. This point may appear obvious to many professionals in family service agencies. But we now have the facts to give a broad-based empirical footing to this view as well as to go beyond that obvious fact and examine the specific character of the changes.

These trends can be explained in several ways. These changes may well be driven more by the availability of funding than by the needs of consumers seeking help. The increase in credit counseling programs springs to mind as one example. Alternatively, defunding of government programs may have driven socially and economically disenfranchised

---

6. Support groups might be appropriate as an *ancillary* service bundled with one of these as primary service.

7. Physical health problems in the 1997 survey were experienced primarily by *non*elderly (87% were younger than 65 years). Therefore, elder care would not be a response well matched to this presenting problem.

consumers into a private sector that was unprepared to meet their needs. In this vein, the service mix documented in 1990 and in 1997 appears to represent an industry that has assembled an armamentarium more appropriate to middle-class concerns of the 1970s and 1980s.

The counterpoint of problems and services signals strategic directions for family-strengthening agencies in the near future. Where dramatic increases in need have not been matched by growth in appropriate services, immense opportunities for expansion are possible. Specifically, because abuse and domestic violence *services* have not grown at anywhere near the rate of these reported *problems*, a significant unfulfilled need appears to exist. The same holds true for child protective services, services for single parents, and, generally, for basic needs issues.

Forces other than the expressed needs of consumers are driving changes in service mix and service method.

Conversely, there appears to be excess capacity in certain service areas, perhaps artificially supported by funding mechanisms. These areas include divorce mediation, health care services, and possibly employee assistance programs. These patterns represent national trends; local program operators must judge whether local conditions override them.

The profile of service plans currently offered at agencies that participated in the 1997 survey is very top heavy, completely dominated by counseling. But the *problems* that consumers confront and report are much more evenly distributed across the limited menu that the survey allowed. Needs and services are therefore grossly unbalanced. This provides the opportunity, and should provide the impetus, for a significant, general diversification of services. The results reported here imply that family service agencies would do well to expand their service offerings generally and to become more flexible and responsive to the problem sets reported by their consumers. The current imbalance of services and problems also suggests that participating agencies need to improve their methods for evaluating consumer needs and how these fit with service plans.

6. THE WELFARE TAG SURVEY

Given the growth in the share of cases manifesting basic needs, it seems fitting to focus on welfare recipients, who are most clearly identifiable with those needs.

An addendum to the 1997 National Survey of the American Family consisted of three questions intended to determine whether the respondents had received public assistance or welfare in the past six months and which of six public resources they found most important. The findings of that addendum, as well as an analysis of the relationship of the recipient and nonrecipient status of respondents to other survey variables, reveals marked distinctions between the needs and resources of recipients compared with those of nonrecipients served by FSA agencies.

Summary findings

■ Among publicly provided resources, recipients of public assistance value *health care* much more than do those respondents who have not received welfare.

■ Recipients of public assistance attach much *less* importance to job training and cash assistance than do nonrecipients.

■ Recipients brought to FSA agencies a distinct set of problems that included a much higher proportion of basic needs issues.

■ Recipients of public assistance rate professional and institutional resources as being much more helpful than do nonrecipients.

The findings discussed below are especially significant because recipients of public assistance or welfare constitute a natural group in the database, which can be viewed as the result of on-the-ground social processes. This distinction is neither *a priori* nor created by the analyst to yield the clearest organization of the data. The recipient versus nonrecipient distinction has a real cultural status comparable to gender. One expects social differences of many kinds to be attracted to and to align with such culturally valid social categories, like iron filings in magnetic fields.

6.1 POPULATION

Of the 7,005 people who responded to the Welfare Tag questions, 33.5% reported having received welfare or public assistance in the previous six months (recipients) and 66.5% reported that they had not (nonrecipients). Not surprisingly, recipients possessed distinct demographic characteristics. They were predominantly single (82.0%), female (76.6%), and White (55.8%). Of recipients, 46.8% were between 18 to 35 years old and 67.8% resided in the city. They typically had a high school diploma or less (80.6%) and were poor (72.8% had a household income less than $12,391 annually); 46.9% were unemployed.

6.2 IMPORTANCE OF PUBLIC RESOURCES

Briefly, consumers who had completed the Assets Inventory (Part II-B of the survey) were asked whether they had received welfare or public assistance in the prior six months. If they responded "yes," they were asked to choose the public resource from a list of six that was most important to them: cash assistance, health care/Medicaid, child care, transportation, job training, and housing. If the consumer checked "no" to the cover question, they were asked to mark which of these six resources *would be* most important to them if they *did* receive public assistance.

A greater percent of recipients of public assistance rated health care as the most important public resource, compared with nonrecipients.

The survey results showed that recipients differed significantly from nonrecipients in the importance that they put on each of these six public resources ($p < .001$ for all resources except housing, which was $p < .05$; see Figure 5). Although both recipients and nonrecipients rated health care/Medicaid most important among the six choices, a far larger percent of recipients (56.1%) than nonrecipients (33.7%) rated it most important. In view of this result, it would seem important to determine the role that health care/health problems play in the lives of those receiving public assistance. In fact, the results of the survey speak to this issue. Far more recipients than nonrecipients reported disabilities

Importance of Public Resources to Recipients and Nonrecipients

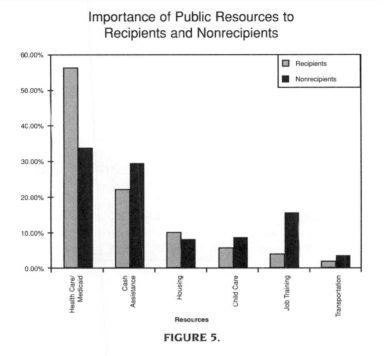

FIGURE 5.

(handicaps) or physical health as problems for which they were seeking service: 6.1% of recipients reported problems relating to disabilities compared with only 2.5% of nonrecipients; 19.4% of recipients reported physical health problems, whereas only 13.3% of nonrecipients did so. The results are significant at $p < .0001$.

Almost four times as many *non*recipients (15.6%) as recipients (4%) rated job training most important. Since recipients are more likely to be unemployed or have low income, with minimal education, one might expect that they would perceive job training as beneficial in pursuing financial independence. However, results from the analysis of resources (below) buttress the conclusion that health issues overshadow concerns about training and skills for recipients of public assistance.

Significantly less importance was assigned to child care (5.7%) and transportation (1.7%) by recipients compared with nonrecipients (8.6% and 3.4%, respectively). Conceivably, the reduced importance of child care in the eyes of recipients might be explained by lack of need as a result of unemployment. Alternatively, recipients of public assistance may place little value on publicly provided child care because they know they have access to this resource through informal sources (family, friends).

6.3 PRESENTING PROBLEMS AND SERVICES OFFERED TO RECIPIENTS AND NONRECIPIENTS

Although Table 6 indicates parenting/child rearing as the predominant problem for both groups, a significantly higher percentage of recipients (31.8%) than nonrecipients (23.6%) listed it as important or most important. The importance of this problem for recipients is reinforced by the 26.2% who reported single parenting as a problem for which they sought help. The evidence uniformly testifies to a *higher level of stress* in the internal family relationships of consumers who have recently received public assistance.

The evidence uniformly testifies to a higher level of stress in the internal family relationships of consumers who have recently received public assistance.

Recipients indicated that basic needs such as having inadequate income (25.5%) and housing (22.9%) were important problems. In contrast, nonrecipients indicated problems in nonessential areas such as social contacts (16.1%), money management (15.5%), and school-related problems (14.1%). Further, the levels of all reported problems are considerably higher for recipients, as signaled by the universally higher percentages of that group seeking help for each of the top five issues in Table 6.

TABLE 6.

Top Five Presenting Problems and Services Used by Recipients and Nonrecipients

Recipients		Nonrecipients	
Problem	**Percent (n)**	**Problem**	**Percent (n)**
Parenting/Child Rearing	31.8% (741)	Parenting/Child Rearing	23.6% (1089)
Single Parenting	26.2% (611)	Abuse/Violence	16.2% (749)
Inadequate Income for Needs	25.5% (594)	In Social Contacts	16.1% (745)
Housing	22.9% (533)	Money Management	15.5% (717)
Abuse/Violence	21.1% (491)	School Related	14.1% (651)
Service Plan		**Service Plan**	
Counseling	63.7%(1485)	Counseling	68.8% (3177)
Support Groups	18.5% (432)	Psychiatric/Mental	14.2% (655)
Psychiatric/Mental	17.7% (413)	Support Groups	12.0% (554)
Child Care	12.7% (295)	Domestic Violence	7.6% (349)
Substance Abuse	10.0% (233)	Credit Counseling	7.5% (344)

Note: Respondents were instructed to check all that apply; therefore a respondent may be represented in more than one problem category.

We compared these categories to the service plans used most often. Although parenting/relationship and nonessential needs are being addressed by appropriate service plans (counseling, support groups, domestic violence, and credit counseling), it appears that the mix of service plans offered to recipients of public assistance may be a poor fit. Specifically, the services offered to this group do not appear to address basic needs adequately.

Job-skills evaluation, job training, and short-term loan programs may be needed by recipients who do not have the ability to meet basic needs. A limitation of the survey was that these particular services were not listed as choices on the menu of services offered. Because 1.8% ($n = 43$) of recipients indicated the use of service plans involving job and debt-management counseling in the "other service plan" category, it is possible that more recipients are using these plans than our results indicate.

The comparison of the resources of recipients and nonrecipients is taken up below, in the discussion of consumer assets.

7. ASSETS OF CONSUMERS

Consumers were asked to complete an Assets Inventory as a means of assessing *strengths*. *Assets* were defined in the instructions as follows:

people, groups, and resources that often are helpful to members of a family in reaching goals, getting things done, or meeting needs.

If the respondent used the listed resource in the prior two years, they were asked to rate that resource in terms of its degree of helpfulness: not at all helpful, somewhat helpful, or very helpful. If they had not used the resource, they were asked to choose an option that explained why: not available, chose not to use, or had no knowledge (of the resource). A menu of 48 resources followed, grouped as family, friends, and other people; groups and associations; agencies; and businesses. The inventory closed with two write-in spaces for "other."

Analysis of data from the Welfare Tag Survey (see section 6) demonstrated that community *resources* are organized by the same social distinctions that organize social life. Few will be surprised by this conclusion, although the implications are profound. But, as noted before, we now have a factual field with a large number of cases from which to argue.

7.1 DIFFERENTIAL USE AND VALUATION OF ASSETS BY DISTINCT CONSUMER GROUPS

In analyzing the survey data, we began by rank ordering assets in terms of helpfulness. We lumped together the ratings for "somewhat helpful" and "very helpful" to arrive at a general sense of whether consumers perceived assets as helpful versus not helpful. This exercise produced the surprising result that the top-rated resources were mostly professional service providers. The result suggested that consumers who had had contact or received services from FSA agencies might be disconnected from family and community resources. However, when we paid more attention to *usage*, in addition to perceived helpfulness, a much richer picture emerged.

All consumers

■ Friends are by far the most frequently used resource among survey participants

■ Neighbors are a resource for more than half of respondents

■ Family members—relatives/kin, parents, spouse, and children—are prominent among the ten most used resources

■ High rankings in terms of use for family, friends, and neighbors contrast with much lower rankings in terms of helpfulness

■ Professional and institutional supports receive higher ratings on helpfulness than family and friends

Table 7 is a top-ten list that displays results for all consumers surveyed and tallies *usage* independently of evaluations of helpfulness. *Usage* reflects the percentage of people who indicated they had used the resource in the past two years, of the total of all answers ("used" plus "did not use") for that resource. (The "did not use" choices included not available, chose not to use, and had no knowledge.) It is immediately apparent from inspecting the rankings that the consumers in this survey are indeed *connected* to a wide variety of resources, including family, friends, and professional help. (The high rate of use for counselor is, in part, an artifact of the survey method, in that contact with a counselor was the most common means of administering the survey at participating agencies.) Table 7 also includes the 11th-ranked resource as a check to see what fell just beyond the cut-off and how close it was to those assets ranked above it.

Friends are by far the most frequently used resource for the individuals and families participating in the survey. The supremacy of friends in the hierarchy of used resources may well be a reflection of the fact that a high proportion of those surveyed were single individuals who might be expected to rely on friends more than consumers who live in households with other related people might be expected to. In what may be cause for optimism about the state of our community life, more than half the respondents also report accessing their neighbors for some kind of support or help. Finally, speaking for the continuing importance of the family, family members occupy four of the top ten slots. Clearly, these people are not disengaged from family support. The story is more complicated and far more interesting.

> *Consumers are indeed connected to wide variety of resources, including family, friends, and professional help. As resources, family, friends, and neighbors are there, but they do not live up to expectations.*

In comparing the "usage" ranking with the "very helpful" ranking, many of the family and community resources fall out of the "very helpful" top ten. Friends falls to 16th place, and neighbors dives to 44th, winning only 21.0% "very helpful" votes from among the 56.3% of consumers who attempted to rely on their neighbors. A higher proportion—29.9%—found their neighbors "not helpful at all" when they sought them out. Own relatives or kin suffers a similar fate, and spouse or partner subsides to 14th place, with a "very helpful" rating less than 50%. Family, friends, and neighbors are *there*, but they do not live up to expectations.

Their places are taken on the roster of the top ten "very helpful" by professional helpers and by service system supports such as day care, preschool, hospital, and charity organizations. Alone among familial assets, parents show staying power, though they are "very helpful" only slightly more than 50% of the time. Mutual support groups make their appearance at the foot of the list. They are the biggest growth area among services offered, as previously discussed.

The resources that consumers regarded as least helpful are those ranked in the right-hand column according to the proportion of respondents who viewed each asset as "not helpful at all." For the most part, these are voluntary associations and clubs, with stepchildren and in-laws thrown in. These resources are also the least commonly used. With the

TABLE 7.

Top Ten Assets: All Consumers
Rank Ordered by Usage and by Degree of Helpfulness

Rank	Total Usage	% Use	Very Helpful	%	Not At All Helpful	%
1	Friends	85.1	Counselor	72.7	Alumni org.	63.5
2	Counselor	77.8	Soc. serv. providers	57.5	Political org.	62.0
3	Own relatives/kin	76.9	Child/senior day care	55.0	Fraternal org.	58.0
4	Parents	70.4	Preschool program	53.3	Ethnic club	52.1
5	Doctor	69.9	Other mental health	52.7	Stepchildren	47.2
6	Spouse or partner	60.5	Hospital	51.6	Sr. citizens' group	46.6
7	Soc. serv. providers	56.4	Parents	50.9	Spouse's relatives	39.7
8	Neighbors	56.3	Doctor	49.3	Landlord	38.1
9	Hospital	52.8	Charity organization	49.2	Outdoor club	37.3
10	Own children	50.8	Mutual support	49.1	Spouse's parents	34.8
11	Other hlth. providers	48.2	Own children	47.8	Godparents	34.7

exception of in-laws and landlord, these assets dwell at the very bottom of our usage rank-order table (see Appendix 4). Spouse's relatives and spouse's parents are resources that are accessed with some frequency (39.3% and 40.1%, respectively) but they are distinguished in this survey as the least helpful familial resources.

Gender differences

■ Generally, women make more use of informal neighborhood assets than men do

■ Men more often use their own parents as a resource

■ Men are more likely to use relationships at work as a resource than women are

■ Women make much greater use of service-system resources, particularly health service professionals

■ Women find professional, systemic supports to be far and away the most helpful assets

■ Generally, men rate social resources of all kinds as less helpful than women do

■ The different patterns of use and valuation of resources that distinguish women from men suggest that social resources play a more critical role in the adaptations of women

Turning to gender differences in asset use, women show a profile similar to that of the general population characterized above.[8] This is due primarily to the fact that women make up two-thirds of the surveyed population. Differences from the total pool of respondents are therefore muted but real. These contrasts are highlighted by comparing women with men (see Table 8).

Women consistently use their relationships more frequently than men do to try to accomplish goals. Women also more frequently turn to their children as a resource. For women in particular, use does not translate readily into helpfulness.

Women consistently use their relationships more frequently than do men to try to accomplish goals. Their frequency of usage for a broad set of informal, neighborhood assets exceeds that of men by two to three percentage points. This set includes friends, own relatives, neighbors, and spouse. Women also frequently turn to their children as a resource

8. It is appropriate to refer to female respondents as women because the Assets Inventory was applied only to consumers age 13 and older and because the age distribution of females who responded indicates that 84% of these were adults older than 18 years.

and do so far more often than men. More women (56.7%) than men (38.8%) have sought help from their children recently. Co-worker replaces own children on the men's usage ranking, signaling their somewhat stronger connection to the workplace and perhaps weaker link to their own families. This notion is supported by the appearance of employers as men's 11th-ranked resource in terms of usage. Of familial resources, only parents are used more frequently by men.

Much stronger contrasts emerge when the use of service system resources is compared. Though the use of counselor is a dead heat between men and women, women make much greater use of health service professionals (doctor and hospital) and social service providers. Schools are another "system" resource that women use significantly more often: 50.6% of women reported having contact with the schools

TABLE 8.

Top Ten Assets: Gender Differences
Rank Ordered by Usage and by Degree of Helpfulness

Rank	Total Usage	% Use	Very Helpful	%	Not At All Helpful	%
			FEMALES			
1	Friends	85.7	Counselor	74.7	Alumni org.	69.2
2	Own relatives	78.6	Child/senior day care	58.6	Fraternal org.	61.8
3	Counselor	78.3	Soc. serv. providers	58.1	Political org.	61.4
4	Doctor	73.7	Preschool program	57.2	Ethnic club	54.4
5	Parents	70.0	Other ment. hlth provider	54.2	Stepchildren	54.0
6	Spouse or partner	62.2	Hospital	52.1	Outdoor club	44.8
7	Soc. serv. providers	58.5	Charity organization	51.8	Sr. citizens' group	44.1
8	Own children	56.7	Mutual support group	50.2	Spouse's relatives	40.6
9	Neighbors	56.4	Parents	49.6	Landlord	37.0
10	Hospital	54.3	Doctor	49.3	Spouse's parents	35.6
11	Schools	50.6	Own children	49.0	Godparents	34.3
			MALES			
1	Friends	83.3	Counselor	68.9	Political org.	61.1
2	Counselor	78.5	Soc. serv. providers	54.1	Alumni org.	55.4
3	Own relatives/kin	74.5	Parents	53.2	Sr. citizens' group	50.3
4	Parents	72.1	Spouse	53.2	Fraternal org.	49.3
5	Spouse or partner	60.9	Hospital	51.2	Ethnic club	47.8
6	Doctor	60.1	Doctor	49.2	Landlord	40.3
7	Neighbors	54.8	Other ment. hlth provider	48.6	Spouse's relatives	37.3
8	Coworker	50.2	Church group	47.0	Godparents	35.7
9	Soc. serv. providers	49.5	Church	46.4	Stepchildren	35.3
10	Hospital	48.6	Mutual support group	46.4	Police	34.7
11	Employers	46.6	Charity organization	45.4	Special trans.	33.2

as a resource compared with 43.4% of men. This may be partly a consequence of women's greater degree of involvement with children, a pattern that pervades the survey results.

For women in particular, *use* does not translate readily into *helpfulness*. All of the familial and neighborhood resources that they reported accessing at relatively high frequencies disappear from the top ten list of "very helpful" resources, with the exception of parents. And parents do not fare well; they drop from fifth to ninth place. With this exception, women in the 1997 survey find professional, systemic supports far and away the most helpful resources. It is noteworthy that 62.2% of women report using their spouse as a resource during the past two years, but only 45.2% of them perceive their spouse as very helpful. This difference between use and helpfulness may be more generally construed as an indicator of the gap between expectation and experience.

Parallel to their generally lower levels of *usage* of relationships to get things accomplished, men also find these social resources less helpful than women. The proportion of men who found the top ten ranked resources to be very helpful is consistently 3% to 5% percent less than women.

Men also diverge from women in the degree to which formal system resources are perceived as very helpful. For men, parents and spouse improve their relative standing when compared with usage. For men, the gap between usage and helpfulness is smaller, particularly for spouse. Further supporting the impression that men find neighborhood assets relatively more helpful than women, church and church group appear in their top-ten list. For women, church and church group rank 20th and 21st in terms of the proportion who found them very helpful. Generally, men find familial and neighborhood resources more helpful than women do and seem to place less stock in service-system supports.

Generally, men find familial and neighborhood resources more helpful than women do and place less stock in service-system supports.

As more women are positive about the most helpful resources, so a greater proportion of them than of men are negative about the least helpful ones. There is a correspondence in men's and women's top-ten lists for resources rated "not at all helpful," but the percentage of women choosing this option is greater for every rank on the list. Women are as a group more polarized in their perceptions of the helpfulness of social assets than men are. Perhaps their lives are more critically influenced by these resources. Data from the 1997 survey support this notion. Fewer women than men are employed, either full time or part time, for example. Moreover, surveyed women have a lower overall level of education. Finally, women are disproportionately represented among recipients of public assistance or welfare in our population. These characteristics describe a group of people who are less able to support themselves as independent economic units for reasons of work, health, mental health, family obligations, or other causes. The apparent consequence is increased dependence on their social resources, leading to attachment to and evident satisfaction with a variety of professional and system supports and concurrent disillusionment with their informal and familial assets.

Differences by household size

■ A significantly greater proportion of larger households has accessed every resource in their top-ten usage set

■ Counselors and support groups are more often seen as very helpful by small families

■ Larger families find schools and immediate family more helpful than do small families

The use and helpfulness of assets can also be studied for households of different sizes. Household sizes reported in the 1997 survey were generally quite small. Few contained more than five members. Household size in this survey probably represents an undercount because many service providers evidently failed to list the other members of the consumer's household when the provider completed Part I of the survey. This conclusion is based on the significant number of survey forms listing only a single individual but in which the consumer's characteristics (e.g., married), problems reported (e.g., single parenting), or the service plan implemented (e.g., child care) individually or together imply the presence of others in the consumer's home.

Table 9 compares relatively small households, defined as one or two members, with larger households, which include three or more individuals. These two classes of households contrast clearly, not in terms of the inventory of resources used, but in frequency of connection with resources. A significantly greater proportion of larger households has accessed every resource in their top-ten usage set. This gap in level of usage ranges from a little more than 2% for friends to 5% for counselor, grows to 11% for parents, and becomes a gulf of 15% for spouse or partner. Larger households also include their own children among their most used resources: 59.7% reported connecting with their children as

TABLE 9.

Top Ten Assets: Difference by Family Size

Rank Ordered by Usage and by Degree of Helpfulness

Rank	Total Usage	% Use	Very Helpful	%	Not At All Helpful	%
	SMALL FAMILIES (1 or 2 in household)					
1	Friends	84.7	Counselor	74.7	Political org.	62.4
2	Counselor	76.2	Soc. serv. providers	58.1	Alumni org.	62.2
3	Own relatives/kin	75.5	Other mental hlth. provider	53.4	Fraternal org.	55.5
4	Doctor	69.1	Child/senior day care	51.7	Ethnic club	51.1
5	Parents	66.5	Hospital	51.1	Stepchildren	49.5
6	Spouse or partner	55.4	Mutual support group	50.7	Spouse's relatives	41.3
7	Neighbors	55.1	Doctor	49.5	Sr. citizens' group	41.0
8	Soc. serv. providers	53.9	Parents	49.3	Landlord	37.9
9	Hospital	51.0	Own children	48.4	Godparents	37.8
10	Coworker	48.5	Charity organization	48.2	Outdoor club	37.6
11	Other hlth. providers	47.6	12-step group	47.9	Spouse's parents	36.6
	LARGE FAMILIES (3 or more in household)					
1	Friends	86.0	Counselor	69.4	Alumni org.	65.9
2	Counselor	81.1	Child/senior day care	59.7	Sr. citizens' group	63.6
3	Own relatives/kin	79.6	Pre-school programs	59.4	Fraternal org.	63.4
4	Parents	77.6	Soc. serv. providers	56.7	Political org.	60.9
5	Doctor	71.4	Parents	53.6	Ethnic club	53.3
6	Spouse or partner	69.8	Hospital	53.1	Stepchildren	43.1
7	Schools	64.2	Other mental hlth. provider	51.5	Landlord	37.9
8	Soc. serv. providers	61.4	Charity organization	50.9	Spouse's relatives	37.4
9	Own children	59.7	Spouse	50.2	Outdoor club	37.2
10	Neighbors	58.7	Doctor	49.0	Spouse's parents	32.1
11	Hospital	56.4	Schools	48.4	Special trans.	31.4

resources, compared with 46.1% of smaller households. In part, we expect such results because large households are more likely to include spouses and children, particularly as we have defined households here. Such reasoning does not immediately account for the great difference in connecting with parents or own relatives, however. These patterns may be correlated with household income, employment status, and even gender differences in the makeup of small versus large households. This remains to be studied in detail in a subsequent analysis of the database.

With regard to gender, it is worth noting that the inventory of resources in the top-ten usage ranking for males is comparable to that for small households, whereas the inventory of women's top-ten resources used is comparable to that for larger households. However, it is not simply the case that men reside in smaller households and women in larger ones. The frequency of connection with the various assets is distinct, most notably for professional supports such as hospital, doctor, and social service providers. *Families*, large and small, make more use of these supports than do men or women alone. Men and small households, on the one hand, and women and larger households, on the other, also differ from each other in the proportion who have accessed their parents in the recent past. Men connect more often with their parents than do members of smaller households. Women do so much *less* often than do members of larger households. This suggests that household size constitutes a significant independent feature organizing the *use* of resources in the communities we surveyed.

Large and small households clearly contrast in frequency of connection with resources. Larger families appear to find more support in their interactions with schools and report more help from immediate family.

Large and small households contrast more in *usage* than they do in how they evaluate the *helpfulness* of resources used. However, in examining Table 9 a few differences do emerge. Counselors are viewed as very helpful by a significantly greater proportion of small households. Mutual support groups are also more often helpful to small families, ranking sixth. Such groups rank 15th (45.5%) for larger families.

Larger families appear to find more support in their interactions with schools. Preschool programs rank 3rd (59.4% very helpful), schools 11th (48.4%), and teachers 17th (44.8% very helpful). The comparable rankings for smaller families are preschool programs 13th (47.6% very helpful), schools 16th (45.8%), and teachers 24th (40.2%). These differences are meaningful and not simply a function of the absence of school-age children in small households, in that they reflect the ratings of only those members of large and small households who reported *contact* with these educational assets. A small portion of consumers' contacts with educational resources results from pursuing their own education rather than that of their children, but the predominant pattern in the surveyed population is contact through children.

Finally, larger families report more help from immediate family than do the members of one- or two-person households. Larger families are more likely than smaller families to view parents as very helpful, (53.6% vs. 49.3%). Of those who tried to use spouse or partner as a resource, slightly more than 50% of consumers in larger families found them very helpful. But only 44.4% of those in smaller households found their spouses this helpful when they sought support. Own children is roughly equal, though it falls from view in the table for large families: 47.0% of those in larger households rated their own children as very helpful compared with 48.4% in smaller households.

The lists of least helpful resources appear similar at first blush. These rankings will be analyzed in a later report.

Use and evaluation of assets by welfare status

- Welfare recipients rely on their available resources with greater frequency than nonrecipients
- Welfare recipients have much greater contact with professional health resources
- Relationships between recipients and certain of their most frequently used resources carry a greater burden than for nonrecipients, women, men, or large or small households
- Resolution of health issues is probably the key to improvement in work-force participation and improvement in the social problems of public-assistance recipients
- Spouses and friends are perceived as much more helpful by those who have not received public assistance

In the brief analysis of the Welfare Tag Survey, we saw that consumers who had used public assistance or welfare in the prior six months had very different ideas about the value of various public resources compared with those who had not used public assistance or welfare. The implication drawn was that these two groups of consumers are distinguished more generally by different patterns of use and evaluation of other resources, notably informal familial and neighborhood assets. That conclusion is strongly supported by analysis of resources in the 1997 survey (see Table 10).

Welfare recipients seem to rely on their available resources with considerably greater frequency than do nonrecipients.

First, with regard to patterns of asset *use*, recipients of public assistance do have access to informal and familial resources in addition to formal system supports. And, according to the Assets Inventory, they do avail themselves of these resources. In fact, as a group they seem to rely on their available resources with considerably greater frequency than do nonrecipients. Reliance on kin, including parents and own relatives, is comparable across the groups. Recipients resort to their spouses less frequently (55.6% versus 60.9% for nonrecipients). However, with regard to friends and neighbors and particularly for professional and

54

TABLE 10.

Top Ten Assets: Welfare Status Differences
Rank Ordered by Usage and by Degree of Helpfulness

RECIPIENTS OF PUBLIC ASSISTANCE OR WELFARE						
Rank	Total Usage	%	Very Helpful	%	Not At All Helpful	%
1	Friends	85.7	Counselor	71.0	Alumni org.	76.2
2	Doctor	81.9	Child/senior day care	60.9	Fraternal org.	70.9
3	Soc. serv. providers	79.2	Soc. serv. providers	59.0	Political org.	65.0
4	Counselor	78.8	Preschool program	58.5	Ethnic club	60.4
5	Own relatives/kin	78.6	Parents	54.1	Sr. citizens' group	52.5
6	Parents	71.8	Hospital	53.9	Stepchildren	51.6
7	Hospital	68.3	Other mental hlth provider	53.5	Outdoor club	47.1
8	Neighbors	63.9	Doctor	53.3	Spouse's relatives	41.8
9	Other hlth providers	62.4	Charity organization	52.2	Informal soc. club	35.2
10	Schools	57.0	Schools	51.7	Spouse's parents	35.2
11	Spouse or partner	55.6	Public transportation	50.7	Godparents	34.9
NONRECIPIENTS OF PUBLIC ASSISTANCE OR WELFARE						
1	Friends	85.0	Counselor	73.6	Alumni org.	57.9
2	Counselor	77.1	Soc. serv. providers	55.5	Political org.	57.0
3	Own relatives/kin	75.9	Child/senior day care	52.0	Fraternal org.	56.6
4	Parents	70.2	Other mental hlth provider	52.0	Ethnic club	50.5
5	Spouse or partner	64.0	Preschool program	51.1	Sr. citizens' group	48.2
6	Doctor	63.4	Parents	48.8	Stepchildren	43.6
7	Coworker	53.6	Mutual support group	48.8	Landlord	40.2
8	Neighbors	51.8	Spouse or partner	48.3	Special trans.	39.8
9	Own children	48.9	Hospital	48.3	Spouse's relatives	39.1
10	Employers	46.4	12-step group	48.1	Outdoor club	35.5
11	Hospital	43.8	Friends	47.7	Spouse's parents	34.9

system supports recipients of public assistance clearly rely on these resources to a much greater degree. For example, 79.2% of public assistance recipients reported using social service providers, compared with 43.3% of nonrecipients.

A startling contrast shows up in the utilization of professional health resources. Doctor, hospital, and other health providers are accessed far more frequently by people who have recently benefited from public assistance in comparison with consumers who have not done so. The comparisons for recipients versus nonrecipients, respectively, are as follows: doctor 81.9% versus 63.4%, hospital 68.3% versus 43.8%, and other health providers 62.4% versus 39.5%. These contrasts are among the largest in use of an asset between major groups of respondents in the entire database.

The portion of a group that uses a particular resource within a given time frame can be thought of as an indicator of the *loading* on that resource. Thus, 85.7% of recipients of public assistance report accessing friends as resources within the prior two years; 86% of larger families also report doing so. As groups, recipients of public assistance and members of larger households may be said to rely more on friends than the other groups of consumers examined here. In these terms, the relationships between recipients and certain of their most frequently used resources—doctors, social service providers, hospitals, other health providers, and neighbors—carry a greater burden than for nonrecipients, women, men, and large or small households. The general pattern is that of much greater loading on system supports and, significantly, on relationships with neighbors. One can only wonder what consequences might follow if the most heavily loaded supports are removed or weakened.

Resolution of health issues may well be the prerequisite to improvement both in work-force participation and in the problems that welfare recipients present at social service agencies.

The contrast in use figures for health resources suggests significant differences in the *health status* of the two groups, consistent with the finding that recipients report health much more frequently as a "presenting problem." It would appear that recipients of public assistance have more reason to access professional health resources because their health status is generally poorer than that of nonrecipients. The results of the Welfare Tag Survey become more understandable in this light.

If this preliminary conclusion bears up under scrutiny, it would imply that policies premised on readiness for work (e.g., current welfare reform) may be overlooking a major reason why these consumers are not already in the work force. If health, rather than will or skill, is a major impediment, it would be more appropriate to concentrate on programming related to health education, prevention, and remediation than on training or retraining. The earlier results regarding the differential valuation of job training and cash benefits also fit with this thesis. Recipients apparently recognize that the major obstacle to their full participation in the work force, and thus to financial independence, is assurance of decent health rather than job training or availability of money. This conclusion further suggests that counselors and social service providers should assess with particular care the health status of consumers who report having used public assistance recently. Resolution of health issues may well be the prerequisite to improvement both in work-force participation and in the problems that these consumers present at social service agencies.

When attention is turned to *helpfulness* of used assets, a clear contrast shines through the thicket of responses. Welfare recipients find formal system supports to be the most helpful assets. Parents also make their appearance among the most helpful resources. In fact, more recipients than nonrecipients find their parents helpful: 54.1% for recipients versus 48.8% for nonrecipients. But *non*recipients also cite a variety of neighborhood resources as very helpful, assets that are lacking from the recipients' top-ten list. These resources include spouse, 12-step group, and, in 11th place, friends. Mutual support group might also be included in neighborhood resources. The fact that in 1997 it became a frequently chosen service plan at FSA agencies may imply that it belongs more with the *formal* service-delivery system.

Spouses and friends clearly perform better for those who are not touched by the welfare system.

Some of these differences are in ranking more than in absolute levels of perceived helpfulness, in that some of the same assets occur lower down in the recipients' ranking but with comparable ratings. This is a consequence of the fact that recipients' high ratings of helpfulness for system resources push nonsystem resources out of the top of the table. For example, mutual support group was rated as very helpful by 48.8% of nonrecipients—7th place. It was also rated as very helpful by 50.3% of *recipients*, but fell to twelfth place, because other resources received higher helpfulness ratings. The 12-step group, rated at 48.1% very helpful and ranked 10th among nonrecipients, checks in at 46.7% very helpful and 17th for recipients.

Spouse and friends are two familial/neighborhood resources that *do* show different patterns. Although 55.6% of recipients report trying to use their spouses or partners as assets, only 43.4% found their partners very helpful (rank 22). The partners of these consumers are rated about as helpful as clergy (also at 43.4%). Spouses are both relatively and absolutely more helpful to those who have *not* received public assistance recently: 60.9% of nonrecipients say they treated their spouses as resources within the past two years, and 48.3% of these nonrecipients found their partner to be very helpful. It appears that the spousal bond is stronger and more helpful for nonrecipients, which is no surprise. The same pattern holds for friends, though usage is more even. Friends are used as a resource by 85.7% of recipients and 85.0% of nonrecipients.

However, they are found to be very helpful by only 42.1% of recipients compared with 47.7% of nonrecipients. Friends clearly perform better for those who are not touched by the welfare system. This raises the possibility that receiving welfare may be associated with the overburdening and breakdown of certain social relationships.

Generally speaking, recipients of public assistance or welfare appear to use all of the resources at their command. In fact, they appear to use all resources at higher levels than do nonrecipients. These facts challenge images of welfare recipients as dependent on the social service delivery system, as lacking in resources or resourcefulness, or as slothful and complacent. Instead, their lives appear to be affected significantly by health issues and by important social relationships in the family and neighborhood that are less helpful than they are for their peers.

7.2 CLUSTERING OF RESOURCES

■ Resources group by patterns of common use into 12 intuitively understandable clusters, the most important of which are *immediate support*, *social life*, and *professional help*

■ The clusters *neighbors*, *own children*, and *library program* pattern as isolated resources, with no clear tendency to be used in conjunction with other assets

■ Weak associations between the clusters *school*, *workplace*, *household*, *professional services*, *neighbors*, and *own children* suggest that community life has become compartmentalized

■ The clusters *immediate support* and *social life* are used jointly by more than 60% of consumers, a sign of the health of family and neighborhood

■ Though on average consumers use a broad variety of resource clusters, neighborhoods have considerable undeveloped potential

■ Welfare recipients are more resourceful than others in terms of using resources from many different functional domains

A deeper question concerned how use of one resource related to use of other resources. Do characteristic patterns of resource usage appear? To understand how resources tracked with each other, we performed cluster analysis on the set of respondents who responded positively or negatively to all 48 resources in the Assets Inventory (a total of 3,932 individuals). The original list of 48 individual resources on the survey instrument allows a very fine-grained view and analysis of the usage and helpfulness of resources for consumers. However, such a long list is also very cumbersome when trying to elicit more general patterns. Moreover, it may contain many individual resources that offer redundant information by virtue of their possibly very close association with other resources. Thus, in order to see the bigger patterns in the data more clearly, a powerful statistical technique known as "agglomerative hierarchical cluster analysis" can be used to sort out internally homogeneous but distinct subgroups of resources, based on the ways in which consumers use or do not use them both as individual resources and in combination with other resources.

First, a measure of distance is chosen to assess how "close" or "far apart" individual resources are from one another, in terms of the way consumers use them. The measures are used to construct a matrix showing the distance between every possible pair of resources. Because the resources are recorded in this survey as "used" or "not used" rather than measured with interval or ratio data, the nonstandardized "binary Euclidean" option was used to measure distance between resources.

The clustering of assets suggests compartmentalization of other arenas in the lives of consumers, notably the relative segregation of school, workplace, household, professional services, extending even to neighbors and one's own children.

Second, clusters have to be progressively formed from individual resources that are closely located on the basis of this distance measure. In this analysis, the "between-groups" average linkage method was chosen for clustering resources. An agglomeration schedule shows the individual resources combining into broader clusters at each step from the beginning (when there are as many clusters as there are resources) to the end (when all resources are grouped into a single cluster). The schedule shows the distance coefficients recording the two most dissimilar points of the clusters being combined at each step.

Third, a choice has to be made with regard to how many clusters will appear in the final solution chosen to represent the "optimal" picture of the data. Given that no single statistically correct solution to the question of the number of clusters exists, this choice can be made in several ways. One way is to examine the step on the agglomeration schedule at which the jump in size of the distance coefficient becomes large, in that large coefficients indicate that clusters with more dissimilar members are being combined at that step. However, in this analysis, no single step yielded a disparately larger jump in comparison with any other step. Given this lack of a natural break, a second, and substantively sounder method was used, which employed a dendrogram, showing the step-by-step progressive grouping of individual resources and later clusters, scaled by the distance at which joins occur. The type of individual resource was examined at each step on the dendrogram to see the points at which the nature of the resulting clusters were substantively changed by the next additional resource or cluster to join. When observed across all forming clusters in this way, the point at which the original 48 individual resources had been grouped into 12 new broad clusters was chosen by the researchers as the "optimal" solution.

After resources are grouped into a smaller number of homogeneous but distinct clusters, the fourth step is to label them in meaningful ways and interpret them. We then use the labeled clusters to elicit larger patterns in the data.

The fact that immediate support is the most used cluster constitutes solid evidence of the continuing importance of family and friends.

At the 11th stage of cluster analysis, we arrived at 12 groupings that had reasonably intuitive readings. These groupings represent the patterns of co-occurrence of assets. In other words, they reveal the tendency of a person using one resource to use other particular resources and *not* to use the rest. We interpret clusters as analogous to *functional domains* in community life. The groupings displayed here are analogs because they do not represent consumers from one neighborhood or community but have been drawn from across the country.

The groupings and the names assigned for ease of reference and intuitive understanding are as follows:

Social life

Fraternal organization	Mutual support group
Sports club/team	Senior citizen's group
Community center	Charity organization
Alumni organization	Outdoor club
Stepchildren	Child/senior day care
Recreation program	Public transportation
Ethnic club	Informal social club
Health and fitness group	Preschool program
Self-help group	Landlord
Political organization	Youth organization
Special transportation (paratransit)	Godparents

Religious life	**Commerce**
Church/synagogue	Neighborhood merchants
Church groups	Lending institutions (banks)
Clergy	Utility companies
Basic protective services	**Library**
Police	Library program
Hospitals	
School	**Workplace**
Teacher	Co-workers
School	Employers
Immediate support network	**Professional help**
Relatives or kin	Other health providers
Friends	Social service providers
Parents	Other mental health providers
Counselor	Doctor
Children	**Neighbor**
Own children	Neighbor
Affines (relatives by marriage)	
Spouse's or partner's parents	
Spouse's or partner's relatives	
Spouse or partner	

Social life, the largest grouping of assets, includes primarily voluntary membership associations, many of which confer or reflect important features of social identity (e.g., ethnic club, fraternal organization). Also included in this group are self-help groups, transportation resources, charities, and stepchildren. Landlord joins in at the fringe of this large set. *Professional help*—health, mental health, and social services professionals— is another clear block of assets used together by consumers. Relatives and kin, friends, and parents are joined by counselor in a set we have labeled *immediate support*. Other groups are *religious community, commerce, school, workplace, affines* (i.e., relatives by marriage), and *basic protective services* (police and hospital). Several resources are used more on a singular basis and are not in as close association with the others. These "isolates" include *own child, neighbor*, and *library program*.

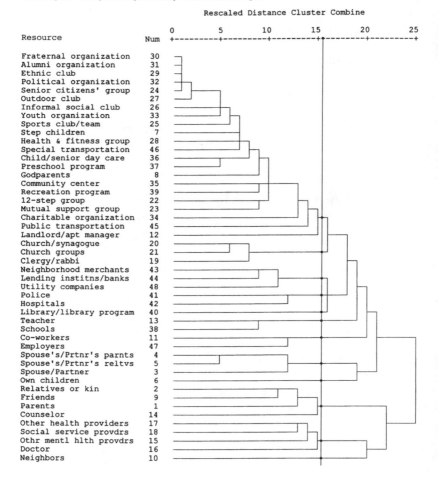

Dendrogram using Average Linkage (Between Groups)

FIGURE 6.

At the next level of cluster analysis, in which resources are progressively lumped by slightly weaker patterns of use, *social life* and *religious life* are joined, and *commerce, basic services* and *library program* fuse together as a block (see Dendrogram, Figure 6). The other categories of resources remain distinct, indicating that the tendency for them to be used together is still weaker. This suggests that neighborhood (i.e., the union of *social life* with *religious life*) is a real, functioning construct encompassing (achieved) social and religious identity. It also suggests compartmentalization of other arenas in the lives of these consumers, notably the relative segregation of school, workplace, household, professional services, extending even to neighbors and one's own children, at least insofar as they are seen as assets.

Consumers who have recently received welfare are more resourceful on average than are other Americans.

We next addressed the frequency with which consumers use resources in the different clusters. This analysis yielded the pattern portrayed in Table 11.

Of all clusters, only the top three are used by more than 50% of the consumers surveyed. The fact that *immediate support* is the most used cluster constitutes solid evidence of the continuing importance of family and friends. Also, that counselor has become the marginal member of this set and that own children are not included suggests unresolved tension and dis-ease in the family or household. Interpreted in light of the clear dominance of *relationships with children* in the problem field (above), this points to broad difficulties in parent-child relationships for which the family is reaching outside itself (i.e., to counselors). This conclusion is

TABLE 11.

Clusters Ranked by Frequency of Any Use				
Resource Cluster	Used		Not Used	
	Number	% of Total	Number	% of Total
Immediate Support	7,301	73.5%	2,637	26.5%
Social Life	6,123	61.6%	3,815	38.4%
Professional Help	5,903	59.4%	4,035	40.6%
Affinal Relatives	4,579	46.1%	5,359	53.9%
Protective Services	5,254	42.8%	5,684	57.2%
Workplace	5,027	40.5%	5,911	59.5%
Neighbors	5,013	40.4%	5,925	59.6%
School	3,873	39.0%	6,065	61.0%
Commerce	3,807	38.3%	6,131	61.7%
Religious Life	3,597	36.2%	6,341	63.8%
Own Children	3,520	35.4%	6,418	64.6%
Library Program	2,840	28.6%	7,098	71.4%

buttressed by the relative importance of the *professional help* cluster, which is more broadly accessed than relatives by marriage, including spouse (affinal relatives). Evidently, older methods for resolving such issues without professional intervention are being abandoned.

Table 11 serves as a rough index of the segregation of resource clusters. If consumers availed themselves regularly of assets in multiple clusters, more of the clusters would rise above 50% usage. Two of the isolates, that is, those resources not linked in patterns of utilization at this level with other resources, bring up the bottom of the table. The exception is neighbors, who, as we have seen, are called on with some frequency by almost all groups of consumers but who are also rated

TABLE 12.

MAJOR RESOURCE CLUSTERS USED IN *CONJUNCTION*

(% of cases using both clusters)

	Social life	Religious	Commercial	Protective services	Library program	School	Workplace	Affinal	Own child	Immediate support	Professional help	Neighbors
Social life												
Religious	32.6											
Commercial	35.3	22.4										
Protective services	39.2	25.0	29.2									
Library program	26.8	17.5	20.5	22.0								
School	35.6	22.1	22.8	26.6	20.3							
Workplace	35.0	21.7	24.8	24.3	18.4	23.7						
Affinal	37.7	22.6	24.1	26.2	18.1	25.0	27.9					
Own child	30.2	18.8	20.4	22.3	15.0	20.4	20.4	26.2				
Immediate support	60.3	35.6	37.5	42.0	28.1	38.4	40.0	45.1	34.7			
Professional help	51.7	31.7	33.6	38.8	25.4	33.7	32.2	35.7	29.5	58.2		
Neighbors	36.6	24.0	24.8	27.2	18.1	25.0	24.4	24.9	21.0	40.1	35.4	
	Social life	Religious	Commercial	Protective services	Library program	School	Workplace	Affinal	Own child	Immediate support	Professional help	Neighbors
Sum of percentages:	421.0	274.0	295.4	322.8	230.2	293.6	292.8	313.5	258.9	460.0	405.9	301.5
Cluster average (% /12):	35.1	22.8	24.6	26.9	19.2	24.5	24.4	26.1	21.6	38.3	33.8	25.1
Cluster rank:	2	10	7	4	12	8	9	5	11	1	3	6

poorly in terms of helpfulness. Neighbors are therefore an enormous potential resource who are currently not effectively linked with the other clusters of assets and who are generally perceived as not very helpful. If the linkage with neighbors can be defined as "neighborhood" then development of neighborhood should be at the top of the agenda of any family-strengthening agency whose consumers share this profile.

To understand the extremes of asset use, we isolated those consumers who exclusively used assets in one cluster. Plainly, few of the clusters alone are capable of offering sufficient support to sustain an individual. Indeed, among all clusters *immediate support* had the largest number of consumers who used only that cluster and no other. But these consumers were a tiny fraction of the surveyed population: only 71 consumers fell into this category, constituting 0.7% of the total pool. Therefore we have

TABLE 13.

MAJOR RESOURCE CLUSTERS USED AS *ALTERNATES*

(% of cases using one cluster and not the other)

	Social life	Religious	Commercial	Protective services	Library program	School	Workplace	Affinal	Own child	Immediate support	Professional help	Neighbors
Social life												
Religious	32.6											
Commercial	29.3	29.7										
Protective services	26.0	29.0	22.7									
Library program	36.6	29.8	26.0	27.4								
School	29.4	31.0	31.7	28.5	27.0							
Workplace	32.3	33.4	29.2	34.7	32.3	32.0						
Affinal	32.2	37.1	36.1	36.5	38.3	35.1	30.8					
Own child	36.7	34.0	32.9	33.6	33.9	33.5	35.1	29.1				
Immediate support	14.5	38.5	36.9	32.3	45.9	35.6	34.1	29.4	39.5			
Professional help	17.6	32.1	30.5	24.6	37.2	30.9	35.5	34.1	35.8	16.4		
Neighbors	28.8	28.6	29.1	28.7	32.8	29.2	32.1	36.7	33.9	33.6	29.0	

little evidence that consumers are able to get by through exploiting resources in only one cluster, at least at this level of cluster analysis.

One can also inquire, having come this far, which resource clusters tend to be used in conjunction with each other (Table 12) and which are used as alternatives to each other (Table 13). *Immediate support* and *social life* are used together in 60.3% of cases, by far the greatest overlap in all cluster crossings (cross tabulations). It is hardly surprising that these clusters would harmonize among these consumers or among any group of Americans. This amounts to a statement of the marriage of informal associational connections with inner family life, which can be interpreted as a sign of the health of family and neighborhood.

Close behind this pairing is *immediate support* and *professional help,* which are jointly used by 58.2% of consumers. More surprising is the conjunction of *social life* with *professional help.* This is the only other overlap that captures more than 50% of the consumer pool. In essence, this pattern indicates that, of people who use resources in the social life cluster, 51.7% also have sought professional help from doctors, other health providers, social service providers, or other mental health providers.

Inspecting the clusters that are used as alternatives to each other (the converse of the conjunction table), the combination that stands out is religious life and immediate support (see Table 13). Of consumers who access resources in one of these two clusters, 38.5% fail to use any resources from the other cluster. This may be interpreted as a measure of the functional overlap of these resource clusters. In other words, the data imply that, to a degree, the immediate family and religious resources (i.e., the religious life cluster) serve some of the same functions in the lives of consumers and are therefore less likely to be simultaneously used by the same individuals.

Generally speaking, the conjunction figures are relatively uniform across this table, with the exception of the isolate *library program.* Most combinations are used jointly by 20% to 40% of the consumers surveyed. This analysis documents that respondents *are* using a variety of resources and simultaneously suggests the existence of many unused resource clusters—a rich field for those social work practitioners who view their work as building linkages and integrating existing resources into their service plans. The potential of neighborhoods, at least in terms of resources, is there to be developed.

Finally, we constructed a table that shows the tendency of consumers to use multiple clusters. We asked, simply, how many surveyed consumers used one cluster, two clusters, three clusters, and so forth, all

TABLE 14.

Number of Resource Clusters Used by Individual Consumers

Number of Clusters	All Consumers		Nonrecipients of Welfare		Recipients of Welfare	
	Percent of Consumers	Frequency (n)	Percent of Consumers	Frequency (n)	Percent of Consumers	Frequency (n)
1	1.6	121	1.8	82	0.8	18
2	3.4	255	4.2	192	1.4	33
3	5.7	431	6.9	317	2.9	67
4	7.1	536	7.9	359	5.5	127
5	9.9	745	10.5	480	8.8	202
6	12.1	910	12.8	583	11.0	253
7	13.4	1014	12.9	588	14.1	324
8	14.1	1065	13.4	611	15.9	365
9	11.6	876	10.7	488	13.5	310
10	9.9	744	8.8	411	12.1	278
11	6.6	498	5.6	255	8.9	205
12	4.6	347	4.4	201	5.1	118
Total	100.0	7542	100.0	4567	100.0	2300
Mean	7.14		6.89		7.72	
Median	7.00		7.00		8.00	

the way up to the maximum of 12. This activity amounts to a measure of how broadly individuals *distribute* their search for resources across functional domains. The degree to which a person uses resources from multiple clusters may be interpreted as *resourcefulness*. The results for all consumers and for recipients and nonrecipients of public assistance are shown in Table 14.

The surprising results demonstrated that consumers generally used an average of seven resource clusters in the course of their daily life ($M = 7.14$, median = 7). Even more intriguing, but consistent with the above analysis of resource use, recipients of public assistance use more resource clusters than do nonrecipients ($M = 7.57$ versus 6.89 for nonrecipients). In other words, as defined here, consumers who have recently received welfare are *more resourceful* on average than are other Americans.

Other comparisons are strongly suggested by the data and will be discussed in future reports. This type of analysis affirms that strengths-based surveys contribute to defining the essential fabric of family life in America.

8. Social Worker Knowledge of Consumer Assets

The questionnaire asked both the service provider and the consumer to check whether the consumer had used any of 48 different potential resources in the previous two years. If the consumer *used* the asset, they were asked to rate each individual resource as either "not at all helpful," "somewhat helpful," or "very helpful." Providers were asked for the same rating on their consumer's situation.[9] The precise wording of the instruction to social workers was as follows:

> A. *If the consumer* **USED** *the resource, please circle the response which best describes how helpful this resource has been to them* **during the last two years,** *on the occasions when they used it.*

Social workers were given one additional instruction, which did not apply to consumers when they completed their own inventories:

> C. *If you don't know or are not sure about the consumer's link to the resource, leave the item blank.*

The two resource inventories then allow the responses of providers and consumers to be compared on the same resource to determine whether the counselor has an accurate knowledge of the resource field being actively used by the consumer, whether the counselor has correctly assessed the helpfulness of that resource to the consumer in the eyes of the consumer, and whether the degree of accuracy varies by the type of individual resource.

We calculated the accuracy of social workers in completing the inventory on consumers by tallying only *nonblank* answers from social

---

9. Social workers were instructed *not* to attempt to complete an Assets Inventory for intake, or first contact cases, and for consumers younger than 13 years. The reasoning on intake cases was that service providers could not possibly have sufficient information about the consumer's assets at their first meeting to complete any of the inventory.

workers. Therefore, instances in which the social worker acknowledged a lack of familiarity with a particular consumer asset were excluded from the tally. Only *attempted answers* are treated as correct or incorrect. This procedure has the general effect of raising the calculated accuracy of social workers in the analysis that follows.

The positive finding is that the counselors are correct on the question of use versus nonuse on all 48 individual resources more than 70% of the time. Averaging across all 48 resources, the providers are correct 83% of the time. At the level of the individual resource, this accuracy varies from 71.8% (for "neighbors") to 94.5% (for "alumni organization").

Less comforting, though, is the fact that counselors are *more* likely to be correct with the *sparsely used* resources, such as "fraternal organization" and "political organization" (which are actually used by only 1.9% and 2.5% of respondents, respectively). Counselors are much *less* likely than the 83% average to be correct on many individual resources that are used by a relatively high proportion of consumers. Social service providers are used by 63% of consumers, but only known correctly by counselors 79% of the time. Other health providers are used by 53% of consumers, but this fact is only known by counselors in 74% of cases. Not even "counselor," used by 82% of all consumers, was in the top-ten list of individual resources correctly cited by providers as part of the consumer's asset field. A number of important familial and neighborhood resources fall into the lower half of the accuracy rankings, including own relatives or kin (81.9% correct), spouse's parents (80.1%), clergy (78.7%), employers (77.7%), and other mental health providers (74.5%). These accuracies should be understood in the context that, given only two choices of "used" or "not used," the service provider is likely to be correct 50% of the time just by chance.

Also of interest is the extent to which providers could correctly assess whether these used resources are perceived as *very helpful* by the consumer. Such knowledge would be key to recommending an effective resource out of many possible alternatives and to not wasting the consumer's or agency's time on resources that have not lived up to expectations. Thus, the same kind of comparison that was done with "used/not used" above can be made with the provider's and consumer's responses to the question about whether each resource that used in the past two years was very helpful or fell somewhere short of this judgment (i.e., *somewhat helpful* or *not at all helpful*).

On this dimension, providers correctly identified the "very helpful" resources, on average, 87% of the time. The range of accuracy by individual resource again varies from 71% (for "counselor") to 99% (for "alumni association"). However, as with "used" and "not used," the highest degrees of accuracy in estimating "very helpful" resources are achieved by providers on many individual resources that are sparsely used by consumers: "alumni association" is used by only 6.3% of all respondents, for example. *Lower* degrees of accuracy achieved by providers came with many resources that were frequently used by consumers, such as "counselor," "friends," "doctor," and "social service providers." This suggests that the providers are less knowledgeable about the helpfulness to the client of the most commonly used resources.

A more finely grained picture, and a far more challenging test, of the provider's ability to assess the helpfulness of the consumer's resources can be drawn by measuring how frequently the provider can exactly match the consumer's own judgment about the *degree* of helpfulness.

Accurate assessment of the consumer's asset field is the logical prerequisite to strategies that attempt change by linking or reconfiguring existing resources.

On this dimension, the ability of providers to gauge correctly was lower than their ability to tell simply whether the consumer had *used* the resource and lower than their ability to identify those resources that the consumer judged *very helpful*. This is not surprising in that knowing the *degree* of helpfulness requires far more intimate knowledge of the consumer's relationships and life. The average percent correct response for all valid cases across all 48 resources was 51.4%. This means that approximately half the time the counselor or service provider could not correctly state the three-valenced helpfulness of a given resource to the consumer. At the individual resource level, success went as low as 27% correct (for fraternal organization). For the best assessed resource, counselor, the rate was 65.4% correct. Generally, providers scored better than 50% correct with 17 of the 48 resources and better than 60% correct with just two (counselor and parents).

This analysis presents a situation ripe with opportunities for family service agencies. These agencies are pressed by many funding sources to achieve higher levels of effectiveness with fewer staff and resources. One economical means of increasing the effectiveness of a small staff is to incorporate the consumer's existing resource network into the service plan. Indeed, that network is *there*. The evidence from this survey extensively documents the depth and variety of resource *usage*, even for groups of consumers whom conventional wisdom portrays as isolated.

If these resources can be effectively recruited to the resolution of the issues for which the consumer has sought help, the potential savings in terms of provider time and prescribed services is significant. The added advantage, of course, is that recruitment of these resources contributes to building neighborhoods. This advantage can be more effectively and quickly achieved if provider assessment becomes refined so that it more nearly matches the consumer's actual field of resources, including judgments of relative helpfulness of these assets. The Assets Inventory or a similar tool can be employed in the tandem fashion demonstrated here to assess the accuracy of providers' knowledge of the consumers whom they serve. The inventory, or a similar tool, can be used alone for consumers to capture their asset usage and how they perceive social resources in their environment. Accurate assessment of the consumer's asset field is the logical prerequisite to strategies that attempt change by linking or reconfiguring existing resources.

9. Synthesis and Conclusion

A sea change in patterns of consumer recruitment to FSA agencies has occurred since 1990. Today, these agencies are serving a consumer population that is more African American, more female, and far poorer than either the U.S. population today or the consumers served at the time of the 1990 survey. Individuals touched by FSA agencies in 1997 also include a very high proportion of single parents, the vast majority of whom are women. Not surprisingly, these people have relatively low levels of education and a shockingly high rate of unemployment and underemployment. More than one-third have recently received public assistance or welfare. The various processes of recruitment to these agencies have selected a group of Americans most of whom have been left behind by the much touted economic recovery of the 1990s and by the social and community development that is presumed to be its partner.

The problems that this transformed clientele confronts and that become the bread and butter of the agencies' business are no longer those of the baby boomers, nor of the Viet Nam era, nor of the Me Generation of the 1980s. The concerns of the middle class have begun to yield to the lifeways of the street at private social service agencies. Social workers are adjusting to the needs of persons with HIV, the unemployed, homeless families, single and teenage parents, felons on probation, perpetrators and victims of domestic violence, in addition to parents who cannot cope with the behavior of their own children.

FSA agencies have experienced a push–pull effect from funding sources, which feeds the present confusion. United Way has reduced the funding for continuing operations that these agencies had learned to expect. Simultaneously, under the new *new* federalism government agencies are contracting with private agencies to provide services to groups of consumers who were formerly served exclusively by public social workers. This environment has tended to polarize the adaptation of agencies. They must choose to compete against many others to deliver clinical and managed care services to more upscale clients or to strike out into the less known world of marginalized people. Some try to have a foot in both worlds. Adaptations are emergent rather than codified or crystallized. This bifurcated adaptational map has led to seemingly odd results, such as agencies offering counseling services to consumers who present with basic needs issues.

This transition has generated disparities between needs and services. Problems are far more diversified than the service responses that agencies have fashioned to address them. Counseling continues as a lone giant among all service options. Moreover, there are strong indications that changes in the array of services are occurring in response to fiscal pressures on agencies rather than in response to the characteristics of clients or their lifeways. This situation has created pockets of unfulfilled need or excess capacity in the service-delivery system, in which growth or shrinkage of consumers' problems have not been matched by adjustments in services.

Popular beliefs and national policy about marginalized people continue to be driven by a preoccupation with their deficits and with the public funds that are expended in attempts to compensate for these deficits. A conventional wisdom has evolved that recipients of public assistance are dependent on the system that serves them, and, the reasoning goes, that work will make them free. These developments in public thought have taken place in the absence of evidence about the *strengths* of these consumers.

The research reported here directly contradicts this current of thought in two ways. First, recipients of public assistance are resourceful, utilizing familial, neighborhood, professional, and institutional assets in their adaptation to a stressful existence. Indeed, the evidence indicates they *use* most of these assets more frequently than people who have not received welfare. They are neither isolated nor dependent on the resources of the formal service-delivery system. However, when they interact with their parents, kin, friends, and neighbors, they receive less help from these relationships than peers who are not touched by welfare.

Second, health is the major issue for these Americans. They report health care as the most valued publicly provided resource. Their patterns of resource use, as well as their evaluation of how helpful various resources have been, suggest that they are experiencing health problems at a far greater rate than the general population. In fact, their health *is* poorer. It is doubtful that job training or placement will cure them of this condition. Until a level of health comparable to the rest of the work force can be assured, work programs will have spotty results.

In terms of family adaptations, the individuals we have surveyed in 1997 are experiencing the *professionalization* of their family life. Though basic needs issues have grown substantially, the problems for which Americans seek help at family service agencies are still primarily those involving social relationships. And chief among these problems are issues involving children. The immediate circle of support in which solutions are hammered out now includes the professional counselor. Moreover, consumers find professional and institutional resources of all kinds considerably more helpful than their families, friends, and neighbors. This inner circle of informal resources therefore has enormous potential for support, which the survey has shown is not now being fully realized. The unevenness in the "helpfulness landscape" suggests that effective and perhaps more efficient social work practice lies along the path of enabling consumers better to use their existing informal assets.

The patterning of assets these consumers use reflects *some* compartmentalization in their community life. Although the consumers surveyed tend not to rely on any single cluster, neither are they disposed to use assets from all of the clusters. Several important informal resources, including own children and neighbors, pattern as isolates without consistent linkages to other assets. Respondents used, on average, 7 clusters from among the 12 functional domains. The observation above regarding the network of informal family support applies equally but more broadly at the community level. The functional barriers that separate clusters of resources and prevent individuals from using all or nearly all of them are an uncharted territory that begs for community-level ethnographic study. Unused clusters represent unexploited potential for consumers and for social workers and agencies that are committed to the internal development of neighborhoods and communities.

However, our knowledge of the asset fields of consumers is imprecise, particularly as to social relationships that are functionally significant. Social work agencies have room to improve in assessing the value of such frequently used resources as friends, counselors, and social service providers. The key to unlocking the power of compartmentalized assets is a more systematic and more refined strengths-based assessment by social workers and facilitators, as well as by consumers themselves.

Appendix I. Methodology

The 1997 survey followed the cross-sectional design used in 1990. The nexus for surveying consumers was their contact with an FSA member agency during a one-week period. In 1990 the survey was undertaken between April 30 and May 5. In 1997, the survey ran from April 7 through April 13. The use of a seven-day period (Monday through Sunday) in 1997, as opposed to the six-day period (Monday through Saturday) used in 1990, was intended to capture the increasing tendency among agencies to provide services seven days per week.

Participating agencies were recruited by personal letter, which went to the executive directors of all 240 FSA member agencies in December 1996. The incentives offered were the opportunity to partake in original research and the promise of a copy of the final report together with an individual agency profile of the consumers they served. Directors who failed to respond received another letter in February 1997. Ultimately, 104 agencies agreed to participate. Fourteen of them dropped out during the implementation of the survey.

The design required the professional staff of each participating agency to apply the survey to every consumer with whom they had professional, face-to-face contact during the survey window. Consumers were to be surveyed only once during that week, in the event that staff had repeated contact with them. Four agencies found they were unable to implement the survey between April 7 and 13 and were permitted to conduct the survey during the following seven-day period, April 14 to 20.

Field testing took place at 20 agencies around the country during February and March. Five hundred draft surveys were distributed to these agencies, and approximately 250 were completed and returned. This process led to significant simplification of Part I and a complete redesign of the instructions printed on the survey form itself. Domestic violence and neglect were added to the menu of problems. Support group was added to the list of service plans. Also, landlord and godparents were added to the Assets Inventory.

Three weeks prior to the survey window, participating agencies were asked to estimate the number of consumers who would be contacted in some face-to-face interaction by their staff members during the target week. Each agency received by mail the requested number of surveys, augmented by 10%, approximately seven days prior to the onset of the survey. The survey was distributed in English. The consumer Assets Inventory, Part II-B, was available in Spanish translation. Agencies that requested Spanish-language forms were provided surveys that included the Spanish versions of Part II-B but in which the parts completed by the service provider (Parts I and II-A) remained in English. Twenty-eight thousand, five hundred surveys were distributed in this manner.

As in 1990, the service provider was asked to provide information on consumer characteristics, their presenting problems, and services offered. This information constituted Part I of the survey. The service provider was also asked *independently* to complete an Assets Inventory on each consumer, based on the provider's prior knowledge of the consumer. Providers were instructed *not* to interview the consumer to obtain answers for Part II-A. The Consumer Assets Inventory, Part II-B, was designed as a tear-off, to be given to the consumer as a self-administered instrument. It was separately stapled for this purpose. All three parts were intended to be completed at the time of contact. As a concession to agencies, Part I could be completed in advance of contact on the basis of prior knowledge or records.

Service providers were given a set of instructions, which appears on the following pages.

1997 NATIONAL SURVEY REFERENCE GUIDE

NOTE: The survey is self-administered, and meant to be self-explanatory. Read the survey forms before consulting this Guide. You may call the FSA Research Department if questions remain after reading the Guide.

Use this Guide by scanning down the left-hand margin for the proper subject.

Purpose:
The general purpose of this National Survey is to take a snapshot of the consumers served by FSA member agencies in 1997. To achieve a cross-section of these Americans, we seek to sample **all** of the groups which your agency has direct, professional contact with and whom you regard as recipients of your services.

Target Population:
Individual consumers who have face-to-face, professional contact with your staff, during the period April 7 through 13, whom you regard as recipients of your services, and for whom delivery of service depends to an important degree on knowledge of their life circumstances and characteristics. In operational terms, these are consumers which your agency **assesses** in some fashion.

Part I: Demographic Instrument

Application: ALL of Target Population, including Intake cases and children.

Completed by: Service Provider.

Method: Can be completed from prior knowledge, files, or by asking the consumer.

Part II-A: Service Provider Assets Inventory

Purpose: To document service provider knowledge of the consumer's resources for comparison with the consumer's account. Coverage: Competed for all ONGOING cases in which the consumer is 13 years of age or older. NOT completed for consumers younger than 13 years, or for Intake cases.

Method: Completed independently by the Service Provider, based on prior knowledge or records. The consumer is NOT to be interviewed to provide this information.

Part II-B: Consumer Assets Inventory

Purpose: To document the resources used by your consumers, their knowledge of resources, and how helpful the resources have been during the last two years.

Coverage: ALL consumers age 13 years and older. This includes Intake cases.

Method: The Consumer Assets Inventory can be separated from the Survey and given to the consumer to complete. It is self-administered. If the consumer needs assistance completing the Inventory, the Service Provider should complete the Service Provider version first, and then provide help. The Surveys do not need to be reassembled, since each part has matching numbers.

Refusal

As with all research, consumers may refuse to participate. In this event, please write "Declined" on the consumer Assets Inventory, but remember to complete the Service Provider portions for that individual. Return "Declined" surveys with all of the completed surveys.

Spanish

A Spanish-language version is available. It is being provided to agencies which have requested it. You may request copies now by calling us. Allow two days for delivery.

Time of Administration

The Survey is to be completed during the Survey week, April 7 – 13. Part I may be completed in advance of contact with the consumer, if the information is known. Part II is to be completed **at the time of face-to-face contact.**

Copies of Survey

Additional copies must be requested from FSA, since they are individually numbered. We will express mail them. DO NOT copy surveys to make up for a shortfall.

Resource people

Thomas E. Lengyel, FSA Director of Research
tlengyel@fsanet.org
Katina L. Jones, FSA Research Analyst
kjones@fsanet.org

Survey #

1997 NATIONAL SURVEY OF THE AMERICAN FAMILY
Part I: Replication of 1990 Instrument
Completed by the Service Provider

A. Case Information

Name of Service Program (*if applicable*): _____

Place of Contact: ❏ *Agency*   ❏ *Community*   ❏ *Home*   ❏ *Other* _____

Status of Case: ❏ *New*   ❏ *Existing*   ❏ *Reopened*

Today's Date: _____ / _____ / 1997   Date of First Contact: _____ / _____ / _____

B. Family Composition and Social Data

1. List consumer first, followed by all individuals living in the household, whether related or not, who consumer considers to be part of their family.
2. If you have face to face, professional contact with other listed family members, please complete a Part I for <u>each</u> of them as well. List their corresponding survey numbers in the column provided (Survey #).

Relationship to Consumer	Age	Gender	Survey #	Ethnicity	Marital Status	Education: highest level	Employment Status	Occupation
1. Consumer		M / F	*above*					
2.		M / F						
3.		M / F						
4.		M / F						
5.		M / F						
6.		M / F						
7.		M / F						
8.		M / F						
9.		M / F						
10.		M / F						

RESIDENCE (*check one*):   ❏ City   ❏ Suburb   ❏ Rural--Town   ❏ Rural--Farm

INCOME:

Total Family Income during 1996 (*before taxes*) from all sources? (*estimate if necessary*) $ _____

What are all of the sources of income received by the family in 1996? _____

_____

C. Service Information

Presenting Problems (Check all problems reported by the consumer and circle the problem he or she saw as most important):

Family Relationships:
___Marital
___Parent-Child (child under 21)
___Other (Specify:_____)

Personality Adjustment:
___Child (under 13)
___Adolescent or youth (13 thru 20)
___Adult (21 thru 64)
___Aged persons (65 and over)

Other Problems:
___Abuse/violence
___Alcoholism
___Criminal or delinquent behaviors
___Divorce
___Domestic violence
___Drug Abuse (Type_____)
___Handicapped
___Housing problems
___Inadequate income for basic needs
___Legal problems
___Mental illness
___Mental retardation
___Management of home
___Management of money
___Neglect
___Parenting/childrearing problems
___Physical health problems
___Problems with leisure time
___Problems in social contacts
___School related problems
___Single parenting
___Step-parenting
___Teen parenting
___Unemployment
___Unwed parenting
___Work related problems
___Other (Specify:_____)
___Other (Specify:_____)
___Other (Specify:_____)

Need for Physical Care or Protective Service:
___Child (under 13)
___Adolescent or youth (13 thru 20)
___Adult (21 thru 64)
___Aged persons (65 and over)

Service Plan (Check all that apply):

___Adoption Service
___Child Abuse/Neglect
___Child Care
___Counseling - Group/Family/Marital/Individual
___Credit Counseling
___Day Care Service for Adults
___Developmentally Disabled/Mentally Retarded
___Divorce Mediation
___Domestic Violence
___Elder Care/Supportive Services to Aging
___Emergency Shelter
___Employee Assistance Program (EAP)
___Family Advocacy
___Family Life Education
___Foster Placement for Children
___Homemaker Service
___Home Health Service
___Hotline/Helpline
___Managed Care Program
___Meals on Wheels
___Plays for Living
___Protective Service
___Psychiatric or Mental Health Clinic
___Psychological Testing
___Resettlement
___Residential/Institutional Facilities
___Service for Persons with AIDS and/or their Families
___Service for Homeless
___Special Service to Minorities
___Substance Abuse
___Support Group
___Teenage Pregnancy and/or Parenting
___Travelers Aid
___Volunteer Friendship Service

All Others _____
_____
_____

Payment (Check all that apply):

___Full   ___Subsidized
___EAP payment   ___Sliding scale
___Third party (non-EAP)   ___Project funded
___No charge
___Other
    Who?_____

If Consumer is 13 years or older, please proceed to Part II.

FSA

Part II-A: Assets Inventory
Service Provider

NOT completed for consumers who are less than 13 years old ⇨ **STOP HERE**
NOT completed for intake or first contact cases ⇨ **GO TO PART II-B**

INSTRUCTIONS: Listed below are people, groups and resources that often are helpful to members of a family in reaching goals, getting things done, or meeting needs. This questionnaire asks you to report your knowledge of the consumer's resources and relationships, and indicate how helpful each one has been to the consumer, **during the last two years**. Please circle the response that best describes the consumer's link to the listed resource.

A. If the consumer **USED** the resource, please circle the response which best describes how helpful this resource has been to them **during the last two years**, on the occasions when they used it.

B. If the consumer **DID NOT USE** this resource during the last two years, please circle the reason which best describes why they did not:

    (4) - if the resource was **not available**, either because it didn't exist, was not accessible, or because the consumer was not eligible to use it.

    (5) - if they **chose not to use** an available resource, for whatever reason.

    (6) - if they **had no knowledge** or were **not aware** of the resource.

C. If you *don't know* or are *not sure* about the consumer's link to the resource, **leave the item blank**.

	RESOURCE USED			RESOURCE NOT USED		
	Not At All Helpful	Somewhat Helpful	Very Helpful	Not Available	Chose Not to Use	Had No Knowledge
FAMILY						
Parents	1	2	3	4	5	6
Relatives or kin	1	2	3	4	5	6
Spouse or partner	1	2	3	4	5	6
Spouse's or partner's parents	1	2	3	4	5	6
Spouse's or partner's relatives	1	2	3	4	5	6
Own children	1	2	3	4	5	6
Step children	1	2	3	4	5	6
Godparents	1	2	3	4	5	6

3

	RESOURCE USED			RESOURCE NOT USED		
	Not At All Helpful	Somewhat Helpful	Very Helpful	Not Available	Chose Not to Use	Had No Knowledge
FRIENDS AND OTHER PEOPLE						
Friends	1	2	3	4	5	6
Neighbors	1	2	3	4	5	6
Co-workers	1	2	3	4	5	6
Landlord/apartment manager	1	2	3	4	5	6
Teacher	1	2	3	4	5	6
Counselor	1	2	3	4	5	6
Other mental health providers	1	2	3	4	5	6
Doctor	1	2	3	4	5	6
Other health providers	1	2	3	4	5	6
Social service providers	1	2	3	4	5	6
Clergy/Rabbi	1	2	3	4	5	6
GROUPS AND ASSOCIATIONS						
Church/Synagog	1	2	3	4	5	6
Church groups	1	2	3	4	5	6
12-step group (AA, NA, etc.)	1	2	3	4	5	6
Mutual support group	1	2	3	4	5	6
Senior citizen's group	1	2	3	4	5	6
Sports club/Team	1	2	3	4	5	6
Informal social club	1	2	3	4	5	6
Outdoor club	1	2	3	4	5	6
Health & fitness group	1	2	3	4	5	6
Ethnic club	1	2	3	4	5	6
Fraternal organization	1	2	3	4	5	6
Alumni organization	1	2	3	4	5	6
Political organization	1	2	3	4	5	6
Youth organization	1	2	3	4	5	6

	RESOURCE USED			RESOURCE NOT USED		
	Not At All Helpful	Somewhat Helpful	Very Helpful	Not Available	Chose Not to Use	Had No Knowledge
AGENCIES						
Charitable organization	1	2	3	4	5	6
Community center	1	2	3	4	5	6
Child/Senior day care	1	2	3	4	5	6
Preschool program	1	2	3	4	5	6
Schools	1	2	3	4	5	6
Recreation program	1	2	3	4	5	6
Library/library program	1	2	3	4	5	6
Police	1	2	3	4	5	6
Hospitals	1	2	3	4	5	6
BUSINESSES						
Neighborhood merchants	1	2	3	4	5	6
Lending institutions (banks)	1	2	3	4	5	6
Public transportation	1	2	3	4	5	6
Special transportation (paratransit)	1	2	3	4	5	6
Employers	1	2	3	4	5	6
Utility companies	1	2	3	4	5	6
OTHER						
_____	1	2	3	--	--	--
_____	1	2	3	--	--	--

Part II-B: Assets Inventory
Consumer

Completed by ALL consumers 13 years of age and older, including intake cases.

INSTRUCTIONS: Listed below are people, groups and resources that often are helpful to members of a family in reaching goals, getting things done, or meeting needs. This questionnaire asks how helpful each of these relationships and resources have been, **during the last two years**. Please circle the response that best describes your connection to the listed resource.

A. If you **USED** the resource or the relationship for some purpose, please circle the number under the answer which best describes how helpful this resource has been to you **during the last two years**, on the occasions when you used it.

B. If you **DID NOT USE** this resource or relationship during the last two years, please circle the reason which best describes why you did not:

    (4) - if the resource was **not available**, either because it didn't exist, was not accessible, or you were not eligible to use it.

    (5) - if you **chose not to use** an available resource, for whatever reason.

    (6) - if you **had no knowledge** or were **not aware** of the resource.

	RESOURCE USED			RESOURCE NOT USED		
	Not At All Helpful	Somewhat Helpful	Very Helpful	Not Available	Chose Not to Use	Had No Knowledge
FAMILY						
Parents	1	2	3	4	5	6
Relatives or kin	1	2	3	4	5	6
Spouse or partner	1	2	3	4	5	6
Spouse's or partner's parents	1	2	3	4	5	6
Spouse's or partner's relatives	1	2	3	4	5	6
Own children	1	2	3	4	5	6
Step children	1	2	3	4	5	6
Godparents	1	2	3	4	5	6

	RESOURCE USED			RESOURCE NOT USED		
	Not At All Helpful	Somewhat Helpful	Very Helpful	Not Available	Chose Not to Use	Had No Knowledge
FRIENDS AND OTHER PEOPLE						
Friends	1	2	3	4	5	6
Neighbors	1	2	3	4	5	6
Co-workers	1	2	3	4	5	6
Landlord/apartment manager	1	2	3	4	5	6
Teacher	1	2	3	4	5	6
Counselor	1	2	3	4	5	6
Other mental health providers	1	2	3	4	5	6
Doctor	1	2	3	4	5	6
Other health providers	1	2	3	4	5	6
Social service providers	1	2	3	4	5	6
Clergy/Rabbi	1	2	3	4	5	6
GROUPS AND ASSOCIATIONS						
Church/Synagog	1	2	3	4	5	6
Church groups	1	2	3	4	5	6
12-step group (AA, NA, etc.)	1	2	3	4	5	6
Mutual support group	1	2	3	4	5	6
Senior citizen's group	1	2	3	4	5	6
Sports club/Team	1	2	3	4	5	6
Informal social club	1	2	3	4	5	6
Outdoor club	1	2	3	4	5	6
Health & fitness group	1	2	3	4	5	6
Ethnic club	1	2	3	4	5	6
Fraternal organization	1	2	3	4	5	6
Alumni organization	1	2	3	4	5	6
Political organization	1	2	3	4	5	6
Youth organization	1	2	3	4	5	6

	RESOURCE USED			RESOURCE NOT USED		
	Not At All Helpful	Somewhat Helpful	Very Helpful	Not Available	Chose Not to Use	Had No Knowledge
AGENCIES						
Charitable organization	1	2	3	4	5	6
Community center	1	2	3	4	5	6
Child/Senior day care	1	2	3	4	5	6
Preschool program	1	2	3	4	5	6
Schools	1	2	3	4	5	6
Recreation program	1	2	3	4	5	6
Library/library program	1	2	3	4	5	6
Police	1	2	3	4	5	6
Hospitals	1	2	3	4	5	6
BUSINESSES						
Neighborhood merchants	1	2	3	4	5	6
Lending institutions (banks)	1	2	3	4	5	6
Public transportation	1	2	3	4	5	6
Special transportation (paratransit)	1	2	3	4	5	6
Employers	1	2	3	4	5	6
Utility companies	1	2	3	4	5	6
OTHER						
_____	1	2	3	--	--	--
_____	1	2	3	--	--	--

Have you received public assistance or welfare in the last 6 months?   ☐ Yes   ☐ No

If **YES**, which public resource is most important to you? Check one:

☐ cash assistance   ☐ child care   ☐ job training
☐ health care/Medicaid   ☐ transportation   ☐ housing

If **NO**, which public resource **would be** most important to you if you **did** receive public assistance? Check one:

☐ cash assistance   ☐ child care   ☐ job training
☐ health care/Medicaid   ☐ transportation   ☐ housing

8

Appendix III. Geographic Breakdown of Returned Surveys

Geographic Distribution of Completed Surveys

U.S. BUREAU OF THE CENSUS REGIONS AND STATES IN FSA SURVEY	PARTICIPATING FSA AGENCIES	COMPLETED SURVEYS RETURNED		DISTRIBUTION OF U.S. POPULATION (1995)	
		(no.)	(% of total)	(no.)	(% of total)
Northeast	36	3,717	37.4%	51,466,000	19.6%
Connecticut		1,288	13.0%		
Massachusetts		46	0.5%		
New Jersey		1,375	13.8%		
Pennsylvania		1,008	10.1%		
Midwest	19	1,685	17.0%	61,804,000	23.5%
Illinois		330	3.3%		
Indiana		143	1.4%		
Kansas		3	0.0%		
Michigan		175	1.8%		
Missouri		72	0.7%		
Ohio		552	5.6%		
Wisconsin		410	4.1%		
South	28	3,946	39.7%	91,890,000	35.0%
Alabama		20	0.2%		
Arkansas		134	1.3%		
Washington DC		121	1.2%		
Florida		248	2.5%		
Georgia		248	2.5%		
Louisiana		43	0.4%		
Maryland		56	0.6%		
North Carolina		915	9.2%		
Oklahoma		223	2.2%		
South Carolina		110	1.1%		
Tennessee		581	5.8%		
Texas		896	9.0%		
Virginia		351	3.5%		
West	6	590	5.9%	57,596,000	21.9%
Arizona		155	1.6%		
California		336	3.4%		
Colorado		99	1.0%		
TOTAL	89	9,938	100.0%	262,756,000	100.0%

APPENDIX IV. RANK ORDER TABLES FOR PROBLEMS, SERVICES, AND ASSETS FOR ALL CONSUMERS

Presenting problems - ranked by percent responding "yes" and "most important"

SPSS NAME	WORDING ON QUESTIONNAIRE	IDENTIFICATION AS A PROBLEM							
		"YES"		"NO"		"MOST IMP"		"YES"+"MOST"	
		(no.)	(%)	(no.)	(%)	(no.)	(%)	(no.)	(%)
FR02	Family Relationships - Parent-Child	3,133	31.9%	6,381	64.9%	312	3.2%	3,445	35.1%
OP17	Parenting/childrearing problems	2,518	25.6%	7,134	72.6%	174	1.8%	2,692	27.4%
FR01	Family Relationships - Marital	1,688	17.2%	7,799	79.4%	337	3.4%	2,025	20.6%
OP28	Other - 1	1,700	17.3%	7,851	79.9%	272	2.8%	1,972	20.1%
OP01	Abuse/violence	1,670	17.0%	8,000	81.4%	155	1.6%	1,825	18.6%
OP21	School related problems	1,618	16.5%	8,110	82.5%	98	1.0%	1,716	17.5%
OP20	Problems in social contacts	1,663	16.9%	8,116	82.6%	47	0.5%	1,710	17.4%
PA03	Personality Adjustment - Adult (21-64)	1,575	16.0%	8,168	83.1%	84	0.9%	1,659	16.9%
FR03	Family Relationships - Other	1,442	14.7%	8,200	83.5%	183	1.9%	1,625	16.5%
OP22	Single parenting	1,575	16.0%	8,216	83.6%	36	0.4%	1,611	16.4%
OP10	Inadequate income for basic needs	1,484	15.1%	8,269	84.1%	74	0.8%	1,558	15.9%
OP15	Management of money	1,358	13.8%	8,432	85.8%	36	0.4%	1,394	14.2%
OP18	Physical health problems	1,249	12.7%	8,468	86.2%	107	1.1%	1,356	13.8%
OP12	Mental illness	1,114	11.3%	8,568	87.2%	144	1.5%	1,258	12.8%
OP09	Housing problems	1,183	12.0%	8,597	87.5%	47	0.5%	1,230	12.5%

Code	Description							
OP05	Domestic violence	1,110	11.3%	8,616	87.7%	101	1.0%	1,211	12.3%
OP02	Alcoholism	1,076	11.0%	8,698	88.5%	52	0.5%	1,128	11.5%
OP25	Unemployment	1,064	10.8%	8,713	88.7%	50	0.5%	1,114	11.3%
PA02	Personality Adjustment - Adolescent or Youth (13-20)	1,023	10.4%	8,758	89.1%	46	0.5%	1,069	10.9%
OP04	Divorce	973	9.9%	8,789	89.4%	65	0.7%	1,038	10.6%
OP11	Legal problems	947	9.6%	8,828	89.8%	52	0.5%	999	10.2%
PA01	Personality Adjustment - Child (under 13)	954	9.7%	8,829	89.9%	43	0.4%	997	10.1%
OP06	Drug abuse	916	9.3%	8,866	90.2%	46	0.5%	962	9.8%
OP19	Problems with leisure time	853	8.7%	8,969	91.3%	5	0.1%	858	8.7%
OP03	Criminal or delinquent behaviors	749	7.6%	9,019	91.8%	59	0.6%	808	8.2%
OP14	Management of home	741	7.5%	9,069	92.3%	16	0.2%	757	7.7%
OP27	Work related problems	722	7.3%	9,076	92.4%	28	0.3%	750	7.6%
PCPS01	Need for physical care or protec serv - child	715	7.3%	9,109	92.7%	3	0.0%	718	7.3%
OP16	Neglect	506	5.1%	9,294	94.6%	27	0.3%	533	5.4%
OP24	Teen parenting	399	4.1%	9,412	95.8%	16	0.2%	415	4.2%
PCPS02	Need for physical care or protec serv - adol/youth	379	3.9%	9,445	96.1%	3	0.0%	382	3.9%
OP26	Unwed parenting	345	3.5%	9,476	96.4%	6	0.1%	351	3.6%
OP23	Step-parenting	336	3.4%	9,478	96.5%	12	0.1%	348	3.5%
OP08	Handicapped	333	3.4%	9,482	96.5%	12	0.1%	345	3.5%
OP29	Other - 2	271	2.8%	9,514	96.8%	42	0.4%	313	3.2%
OP13	Mental retardation	254	2.6%	9,563	97.3%	9	0.1%	263	2.7%
PCPS04	Need for physical care or protec serv - aged	204	2.1%	9,604	97.7%	19	0.2%	223	2.3%
PA04	Personality Adjustment - Aged persons (65 & over)	195	2.0%	9,628	98.0%	4	0.0%	199	2.0%
PCPS03	Need for physical care or protec serv - adult	183	1.9%	9,642	98.1%	2	0.0%	185	1.9%
OP30	Other - 3	58	0.6%	9,759	99.3%	9	0.1%	67	0.7%

Service plan responses, 1990 and 1997
- ranked in order of % frequency responding "Yes"

1990 "AMERICAN FAMILIES IN TROUBLE"

SERVICE PLAN	"YES"		"NO"		TOT
(wording as on questionnaire - respondents could check all that apply)	(no.)	(% of those answering this SP option)	(no.)	(% of those answering this SP option)	(no.)
SP04 Counslng - Grp/Fam/Mar/Indiv	11,902	72.4%	4,540	27.6%	16,442
SP23 Psychiatric or mental health clinic	2,378	14.5%	14,067	85.5%	16,445
SP30 Substance abuse	1,665	10.1%	14,780	89.9%	16,445
SP35 "Others" - 1	1,385	8.6%	14,732	91.4%	16,117
SP02 Child abuse/neglect	1,296	7.9%	15,147	92.1%	16,443
SP16 Homemaker service	1,274	7.7%	15,171	92.3%	16,445
SP14 Family life education	1,214	7.4%	15,231	92.6%	16,445
SP09 Domestic violence	1,133	6.9%	15,310	93.1%	16,443
SP10 Elder care/supprtve servs to aging	1,123	6.8%	15,322	93.2%	16,445
SP24 Psychological testing	824	5.0%	15,621	95.0%	16,445
SP05 Credit counseling	719	4.4%	15,725	95.6%	16,444
SP03 Child care	650	4.0%	15,795	96.0%	16,445
SP22 Protective service	642	3.9%	15,803	96.1%	16,445
SP26 Residential/Institutional facilities	626	3.8%	15,819	96.2%	16,445
SP17 Home health service	568	3.5%	15,877	96.5%	16,445
SP13 Family advocacy	523	3.2%	15,922	96.8%	16,445
SP15 Foster placement for children	428	2.6%	16,017	97.4%	16,445
SP19 Managed care program	426	2.6%	16,019	97.4%	16,445
SP36 "Others" - 2	391	2.4%	15,963	97.6%	16,354
SP32 Teenage pregnancy and/or parenting	388	2.4%	16,057	97.6%	16,445
SP20 Meals on wheels	354	2.2%	16,091	97.8%	16,445
SP34 Volunteer friendship service	348	2.1%	16,097	97.9%	16,445
SP12 Employee assistance prog (EAP)	346	2.1%	16,099	97.9%	16,445
SP18 Hotline/helpline	328	2.0%	16,117	98.0%	16,445
SP25 Resettlement	317	1.9%	16,128	98.1%	16,445
SP08 Divorce mediation	305	1.9%	16,140	98.1%	16,445
SP07 Devlpmntlly disabld/ment retrded	300	1.8%	16,145	98.2%	16,445
SP11 Emergency shelter	298	1.8%	16,147	98.2%	16,445
SP29 Special service to minorities	201	1.2%	16,244	98.8%	16,445
SP06 Day care service for adults	193	1.2%	16,252	98.8%	16,445
SP01 Adoption service	192	1.2%	16,253	98.8%	16,445
SP28 Service for homeless	133	0.8%	16,312	99.2%	16,445
SP37 "Others" - 3	124	0.8%	16,321	99.2%	16,445
SP27 Servs fr prsns w AIDS &/or their fams	33	0.2%	16,412	99.8%	16,445
SP33 Travelers aid	16	0.1%	16,429	99.9%	16,445
SP21 Plays for living	12	0.1%	16,433	99.9%	16,445
SP31 Support group		0.0%			

| Service plan responses, 1990 and 1997 — ranked in order of % frequency responding "Yes" | | | | |

SERVICE PLAN	"YES"		"NO"		TOT
(wording as on questionnaire - respondents could check all that apply)	(no.)	(% of those answering this SP option)	(no.)	(% of those answering this SP option)	(no.)
SP04 Counslng - Grp/Fam/Mar/Indiv	6,560	**66.0%**	3,267	32.9%	9,938
SP23 Psychiatric or mental health clinic	1,443	**14.5%**	8,384	84.4%	9,938
SP31 Support group	1,327	**13.4%**	8,500	85.5%	9,938
SP35 "Others" - 1	934	**9.4%**	0	0.0%	9,938
SP03 Child care	793	**8.0%**	9,034	90.9%	9,938
SP09 Domestic violence	744	**7.5%**	9,083	91.4%	9,938
SP30 Substance abuse	744	**7.5%**	9,083	91.4%	9,938
SP13 Family advocacy	593	**6.0%**	9,234	92.9%	9,938
SP02 Child abuse/neglect	583	**5.9%**	9,243	93.0%	9,938
SP14 Family life education	564	**5.7%**	9,263	93.2%	9,938
SP05 Credit counseling	547	**5.5%**	9,279	93.4%	9,938
SP24 Psychological testing	534	**5.4%**	9,292	93.5%	9,938
SP15 Foster placement for children	454	**4.6%**	9,373	94.3%	9,938
SP16 Homemaker service	430	**4.3%**	9,397	94.6%	9,938
SP22 Protective service	379	**3.8%**	9,448	95.1%	9,938
SP10 Elder care/supprtve servs to aging	306	**3.1%**	9,521	95.8%	9,938
SP26 Residential/Institutional facilities	296	**3.0%**	9,531	95.9%	9,938
SP18 Hotline/helpline	289	**2.9%**	9,538	96.0%	9,938
SP17 Home health service	269	**2.7%**	9,558	96.2%	9,938
SP32 Teenage pregnancy and/or parenting	266	**2.7%**	9,559	96.2%	9,938
SP07 Devlpmntlly disabld/ment retrded	232	**2.3%**	9,595	96.5%	9,938
SP12 Employee assistance prog (EAP)	219	**2.2%**	9,607	96.7%	9,938
SP11 Emergency shelter	207	**2.1%**	9,620	96.8%	9,938
SP01 Adoption service	183	**1.8%**	9,644	97.0%	9,938
SP06 Day care service for adults	182	**1.8%**	9,645	97.1%	9,938
SP19 Managed care program	164	**1.7%**	9,663	97.2%	9,938
SP25 Resettlement	158	**1.6%**	9,669	97.3%	9,938
SP28 Service for homeless	150	**1.5%**	9,676	97.4%	9,938
SP08 Divorce mediation	144	**1.4%**	9,683	97.4%	9,938
SP20 Meals on wheels	131	**1.3%**	9,696	97.6%	9,938
SP27 Servs fr prsns w AIDS &/or their fams	130	**1.3%**	9,697	97.6%	9,938
SP36 "Others" - 2	126	**1.3%**	0	0.0%	9,938
SP34 Volunteer friendship service	121	**1.2%**	9,705	97.7%	9,938
SP29 Special service to minorities	106	**1.1%**	9,721	97.8%	9,938
SP37 "Others" - 3	37	**0.4%**	0	0.0%	9,938
SP21 Plays for living	23	**0.2%**	9,804	98.7%	9,938
SP33 Travelers aid	16	**0.2%**	9,810	98.7%	9,938

Resources ranked for all respondents by percent "very helpful"

RESOURCE	RESPONSE									
	"NOT AT ALL HELPFUL"		"SOMEWHAT HELPFUL"		"VERY HELPFUL"		TOTAL RESPONSES		"SOMEWHAT" & "VERY" AS SHARE OF TOTAL	
	(no.)	(%)	(no.)	(%)	(no.)	(%)	(no.)	(%)	(no.)	(%)
Counselor	230	4.2%	1,270	23.1%	4,000	72.7%	5,500	100.0%	5,270	95.8%
Social service providers	436	11.1%	1,226	31.3%	2,251	57.5%	3,913	100.0%	3,477	88.9%
Child or senior day care	249	19.2%	336	25.8%	715	55.0%	1,300	100.0%	1,051	80.8%
Pre-school program	265	21.9%	300	24.8%	644	53.3%	1,209	100.0%	944	78.1%
Other mental health providers	371	11.8%	1,117	35.5%	1,655	52.7%	3,143	100.0%	2,772	88.2%
Hospital	362	10.0%	1,395	38.4%	1,874	51.6%	3,631	100.0%	3,269	90.0%
Parents	628	12.3%	1,872	36.7%	2,596	50.9%	5,096	100.0%	4,468	87.7%
Doctor	435	8.8%	2,067	41.9%	2,431	49.3%	4,933	100.0%	4,498	91.2%
Charity organization	302	13.3%	855	37.5%	1,122	49.2%	2,279	100.0%	1,977	86.7%
Mutual support group	271	16.0%	591	34.9%	830	49.1%	1,692	100.0%	1,421	84.0%
Own children	459	13.0%	1,377	39.1%	1,684	47.8%	3,520	100.0%	3,061	87.0%
Schools	381	11.7%	1,340	41.3%	1,522	46.9%	3,243	100.0%	2,862	88.3%
Step group	321	23.2%	415	30.1%	645	46.7%	1,381	100.0%	1,060	76.8%
Partner or spouse partner	814	19.6%	1,405	33.8%	1,940	46.6%	4,159	100.0%	3,345	80.4%
Transportation	347	15.3%	868	38.3%	1,051	46.4%	2,266	100.0%	1,919	84.7%
Friends	423	6.8%	2,961	47.6%	2,835	45.6%	6,219	100.0%	5,796	93.2%
Church group	370	15.0%	977	39.6%	1,121	45.4%	2,468	100.0%	2,098	85.0%
Other health providers	421	13.0%	1,355	41.9%	1,460	45.1%	3,236	100.0%	2,815	87.0%
Church	395	13.0%	1,275	42.1%	1,362	44.9%	3,032	100.0%	2,637	87.0%
Special transportation	342	29.8%	293	25.5%	513	44.7%	1,148	100.0%	806	70.2%

Library or library programs	292	10.3%	1,309	46.1%	1,239	43.6%	2,840	100.0%	2,548	89.7%
Recreation programs	241	13.8%	756	43.3%	749	42.9%	1,746	100.0%	1,505	86.2%
Teachers	448	15.7%	1,207	42.2%	1,205	42.1%	2,860	100.0%	2,412	84.3%
Community center	279	17.3%	668	41.4%	668	41.4%	1,615	100.0%	1,336	82.7%
Clergy	445	18.2%	999	40.8%	1,004	41.0%	2,448	100.0%	2,003	81.8%
Sports club or team	279	23.3%	443	37.0%	475	39.7%	1,197	100.0%	918	76.7%
Youth organization	251	22.6%	423	38.0%	439	39.4%	1,113	100.0%	862	77.4%
Health and fitness group	261	20.1%	538	41.4%	500	38.5%	1,299	100.0%	1,038	79.9%
Employers	491	17.1%	1,279	44.5%	1,102	38.4%	2,872	100.0%	2,381	82.9%
Own relatives or kin	781	14.1%	2,655	48.1%	2,084	37.8%	5,520	100.0%	4,739	85.9%
Godparents	385	34.7%	365	32.9%	360	32.4%	1,110	100.0%	725	65.3%
Police	775	26.0%	1,250	42.0%	951	32.0%	2,976	100.0%	2,201	74.0%
Utility company	649	25.5%	1,124	44.1%	774	30.4%	2,547	100.0%	1,898	74.5%
Neighborhood merchants	559	22.6%	1,170	47.2%	749	30.2%	2,478	100.0%	1,919	77.4%
Informal social club	284	27.7%	433	42.3%	307	30.0%	1,024	100.0%	740	72.3%
Lending institutions or banks	747	28.3%	1,118	42.3%	775	29.4%	2,640	100.0%	1,893	71.7%
Outdoor club	255	37.3%	233	34.1%	195	28.6%	683	100.0%	428	62.7%
Coworker	621	19.2%	1,711	52.8%	907	28.0%	3,239	100.0%	2,618	80.8%
Spouse's or partner's parents	971	34.8%	1,079	38.7%	739	26.5%	2,789	100.0%	1,818	65.2%
Landlord	897	38.1%	858	36.5%	598	25.4%	2,353	100.0%	1,456	61.9%
Senior citizens group	275	46.6%	168	28.5%	147	24.9%	590	100.0%	315	53.4%
Step children	366	47.2%	230	29.6%	180	23.2%	776	100.0%	410	52.8%
Ethnic group	280	52.1%	138	25.7%	119	22.2%	537	100.0%	257	47.9%
Neighbors	1,201	29.9%	1,970	49.1%	842	21.0%	4,013	100.0%	2,812	70.1%
Spouse's or partner's relatives	1,086	39.7%	1,092	39.9%	560	20.5%	2,738	100.0%	1,652	60.3%
Fraternal organization	271	58.0%	122	26.1%	74	15.8%	467	100.0%	196	42.0%
Political organization	324	62.0%	135	25.8%	64	12.2%	523	100.0%	199	38.0%
Alumni organization	278	63.5%	107	24.4%	53	12.1%	438	100.0%	160	36.5%

Shares of respondents reporting usage of different resources (1+2+3 as % of 1+2+3+4+5+6) - ranked

ALL RESPONDENTS		MALES		FEMALES	
RESOURCE	USE (%)	RESOURCE	USE (%)	RESOURCE	USE (%)
Friends	85.1	Friends	83.3	Friends	85.7
Counselor	77.8	Counselor	78.5	Own relatives or kin	78.6
Own relatives or kin	76.9	Own relatives or kin	74.5	Counselor	78.3
Parents	70.4	Parents	72.1	Doctor	73.7
Doctor	69.9	Spouse/partner	60.9	Parents	70.0
Spouse/partner	60.5	Doctor	60.1	Spouse/partner	62.2
Social service providers	56.4	Neighbors	54.8	Social service providers	58.5
Neighbors	56.3	Coworker	50.2	Own children	56.7
Hospital	52.8	Social service providers	49.5	Neighbors	56.4
Own children	50.8	Hospital	48.6	Hospital	54.3
Other health providers	48.2	Employers	46.6	Schools	50.6
Coworker	47.8	Oth mentl hlth provdrs	44.0	Other health providers	50.3
Schools	47.7	Schools	43.4	Oth mentl hlth provdrs	47.3
Oth mentl hlth provdrs	46.2	Police	42.6	Coworker	46.7
Police	43.6	Other health providers	41.5	Church	45.0
Church	43.4	Teachers	40.8	Police	44.0
Employers	43.1	Church	40.4	Library or library progs	42.8
Teachers	42.1	Library or library progs	39.3	Teachers	42.5
Library or library progs	41.7	Spouse's/partner's parents	38.8	Spouse's/partner's parents	42.0
Spouse's/partner's parents	40.1	Own children	38.8	Spouse's/partner's reltvs	41.6
Spouse's/partner's reltvs	39.3	Lending institns/banks	38.1	Employers	41.6
Lending institns/banks	39.0	Spouse's/partner's reltvs	36.5	Utility company	40.2
Utility company	38.7	Utility company	36.3	Lending institns/banks	40.0
Neighborhood merchants	36.8	Neighborhood merchants	36.0	Neighborhood merchants	37.6
Clergy	36.2	Clergy	33.6	Clergy	37.0
Church group	35.7	Church group	33.1	Church group	36.9
Landlord	34.9	Transportation	31.8	Landlord	36.4
Transportation	33.5	Landlord	30.3	Charity organization	35.1
Charity organization	33.3	Charity organization	29.8	Transportation	33.5
Recreation programs	26.2	Recreation programs	27.6	Recreation programs	25.7
Mutual support group	25.0	Sports club or team	23.7	Mutual support group	25.1
Community center	23.8	Mutual support group	23.5	Community center	24.3
Step group	20.6	Community center	22.1	Child or senior day care	21.9
Child or senior day care	19.6	Step group	21.7	Pre-school program	20.9
Health and fitness group	19.3	Health and fitness group	19.5	Step group	19.2
Pre-school program	18.5	Youth organization	16.8	Health and fitness group	19.2
Sports club or team	17.9	Informal social club	16.0	Special transportation	17.6
Special transportation	17.4	Godparents	15.3	Godparents	17.4
Godparents	17.0	Pre-school program	15.3	Youth organization	16.5
Youth organization	16.7	Special transportation	14.7	Sports club or team	14.7
Informal social club	15.3	Child or senior day care	14.5	Informal social club	14.7
Step children	12.3	Step children	13.6	Step children	11.7
Outdoor club	10.3	Outdoor club	12.4	Senior citizens group	8.9
Senior citizens group	9.0	Ethnic club	8.7	Outdoor club	8.7
Ethnic club	8.0	Senior citizens group	8.6	Political organization	7.7
Political organization	7.9	Fraternal organization	8.0	Ethnic club	7.6
Fraternal organization	7.1	Political organization	7.8	Fraternal organization	6.3
Alumni organization	6.6	Alumni organization	7.0	Alumni organization	5.9

Shares of respondents reporting usage of different resources (1+2+3 as % of 1+2+3+4+5+6) - ranked

SMALL FAMILIES		LARGE FAMILES	
RESOURCE	USE (%)	RESOURCE	USE (%)
Friends	84.7	Friends	86.0
Counselor	76.2	Counselor	81.1
Own relatives or kin	75.5	Own relatives or kin	79.6
Doctor	69.1	Parents	77.6
Parents	66.5	Doctor	71.4
Spouse/partner	55.4	Spouse/partner	69.8
Neighbors	55.1	Schools	64.2
Social service providers	53.9	Social service providers	61.4
Hospital	51.0	Own children	59.7
Coworker	48.5	Neighbors	58.7
Other health providers	47.6	Hospital	56.4
Own children	46.1	Teachers	54.7
Oth mentl hlth provdrs	45.5	Police	50.2
Church	43.2	Other health providers	49.1
Employers	43.0	Spouse's/partner's parents	48.0
Police	40.1	Oth mentl hlth provdrs	47.8
Lending institns/banks	39.8	Spouse's/partner's reltvs	47.4
Library or library progs	39.5	Coworker	45.8
Schools	38.8	Library or library progs	45.8
Utility company	38.4	Church	44.1
Neighborhood merchants	37.0	Employers	43.1
Clergy	36.2	Utility company	39.3
Landlord	35.7	Lending institns/banks	37.5
Spouse's/partner's parents	35.6	Church group	36.8
Teachers	35.2	Neighborhood merchants	36.4
Church group	35.1	Clergy	36.2
Spouse's/partner's reltvs	34.8	Charity organization	35.0
Transportation	33.3	Transportation	34.1
Charity organization	32.6	Landlord	33.4
Mutual support group	26.3	Recreation programs	32.4
Recreation programs	22.9	Community center	26.2
Community center	22.6	Pre-school program	25.7
Step group	21.5	Child or senior day care	24.0
Health and fitness group	20.0	Mutual support group	22.7
Special transportation	17.7	Youth organization	22.1
Child or senior day care	17.3	Godparents	21.8
Sports club or team	16.2	Sports club or team	20.9
Informal social club	15.9	Step group	18.8
Pre-school program	14.6	Health and fitness group	17.9
Godparents	14.5	Special transportation	16.7
Youth organization	13.8	Informal social club	14.1
Step children	11.5	Step children	13.7
Senior citizens group	10.4	Outdoor club	9.8
Outdoor club	10.4	Ethnic club	8.0
Political organization	8.3	Political organization	7.1
Ethnic club	8.0	Senior citizens group	6.3
Fraternal organization	7.4	Fraternal organization	6.3
Alumni organization	6.9	Alumni organization	5.8

Shares of respondents reporting usage of different resources (1+2+3 as % of 1+2+3+4+5+6) - ranked

RECIPIENTS		NON-RECIPIENTS	
RESOURCE	USE (%)	RESOURCE	USE (%)
Friends	85.7	Friends	85.0
Doctor	81.9	Counselor	77.1
Social service providers	79.2	Own relatives or kin	75.9
Counselor	78.8	Parents	70.2
Own relatives or kin	78.6	Spouse/partner	64.0
Parents	71.8	Doctor	63.4
Hospital	68.3	Coworker	53.6
Neighbors	63.9	Neighbors	51.8
Other health providers	62.4	Own children	48.9
Schools	57.0	Employers	46.4
Spouse/partner	55.6	Hospital	43.8
Own children	55.2	Social service providers	43.3
Oth mentl hlth provdrs	54.7	Schools	42.8
Police	52.8	Church	41.9
Teachers	50.0	Oth mentl hlth provdrs	40.3
Landlord	48.6	Spouse's/partner's parents	39.9
Transportation	48.6	Other health providers	39.5
Library or library progs	48.5	Lending institns/banks	38.9
Utility company	46.7	Spouse's/partner's reltvs	38.8
Charity organization	45.5	Police	38.3
Church	44.8	Library or library progs	38.0
Neighborhood merchants	41.9	Teachers	37.3
Spouse's/partner's parents	41.0	Utility company	34.4
Spouse's/partner's reltvs	40.6	Clergy	34.1
Lending institns/banks	39.2	Neighborhood merchants	33.4
Clergy	38.9	Church group	33.0
Church group	38.8	Landlord	26.6
Coworker	36.1	Charity organization	25.9
Employers	35.9	Transportation	24.6
Community center	31.0	Recreation programs	23.0
Recreation programs	29.6	Mutual support group	21.6
Mutual support group	28.3	Step group	19.0
Child or senior day care	27.1	Health and fitness group	18.9
Special transportation	27.0	Community center	18.4
Pre-school program	24.2	Sports club or team	17.6
Step group	22.6	Child or senior day care	15.1
Godparents	20.0	Pre-school program	15.1
Youth organization	19.1	Godparents	14.6
Health and fitness group	17.8	Youth organization	14.5
Sports club or team	15.8	Informal social club	14.4
Informal social club	14.9	Step children	12.3
Step children	11.5	Special transportation	11.4
Outdoor club	10.0	Outdoor club	9.1
Senior citizens group	9.9	Senior citizens group	7.0
Ethnic club	8.9	Ethnic club	6.7
Political organization	8.7	Political organization	6.5
Fraternal organization	7.4	Alumni organization	5.9
Alumni organization	7.0	Fraternal organization	5.8

Appendix V. Agencies Participating in the National Survey

District of Columbia

Florida

Georgia

Illinois

Indiana

Kansas

Louisiana

Maryland

Massachusetts

Michigan

Missouri

New Jersey

North Carolina

Ohio

Oklahoma

Pennsylvania

South Carolina

Tennessee

Texas

Virginia

Wisconsin